LOVE'S NEW EARTH

Awakening to our Collective True Nature as Love.
-with Rays of Hope and Reasons to Prevail-

Hope Ives Mauran

BALBOA.PRESS
A DIVISION OF HAY HOUSE

Copyright © 2024 Hope Ives Mauran.

All rights reserved. References, quotes and citations must be attributed to their original authors. This book may be reproduced, transmitted or utilized in any form by any means including photocopying, for personal or non-commercial use, without permission in writing from the author. There are no restrictions except word changes and changes to the text are not allowed.

Balboa Press books may be ordered through booksellers or by contacting:

Balboa Press
A Division of Hay House
1663 Liberty Drive
Bloomington, IN 47403
www.balboapress.com
844-682-1282

Because of the dynamic nature of the Internet, any web addresses or links contained in this book may have changed since publication and may no longer be valid. The views expressed in this work are solely those of the author and do not necessarily reflect the views of the publisher, and the publisher hereby disclaims any responsibility for them.

The author of this book does not dispense medical advice or prescribe the use of any technique as a form of treatment for physical, emotional, or medical problems without the advice of a physician, either directly or indirectly. The intent of the author is only to offer information of a general nature to help you in your quest for emotional and spiritual well-being. In the event you use any of the information in this book for yourself, which is your constitutional right, the author and the publisher assume no responsibility for your actions.

Interior Graphics/Art Credits: Hope Ives Mauran; Glove photo by Ross Newkirk; Author Photo by BARRIE FISHER PHOTO

Front Cover by Michael Stack of Sacred Mountain Multidimensional Media using Author's artwork: The Future is Positive, acrylic and gold leaf, 12" x 48"

The old Earth, captured in the net of darkness is lifted and transformed, freed and enlightened, by 6 bright lights who have come to Earth to assist at this time in catalyzing the creation of Love's New Earth.

Print information available on the last page.

ISBN: 979-8-7652-5038-9 (sc)
ISBN: 979-8-7652-5037-2 (e)

Library of Congress Control Number: 2024905239

Balboa Press rev. date: 04/16/2024

CONTENTS

DEDICATION IX
OVERVIEW XI
CH I TRUST THAT LOVE IS ALL AROUND US 1
   Sarah's Package 1
   The Field of Love 4
   Ben and the Gang 5
   Ross' Grace 7
   More Evidence for The Field of Love 9
   A Light In the Head 15
   A Mass Awakening 20

CH II ALL ONE CONSCIOUSNESS 25
   Sam's Subway Ride 25
   Who Are We? 27
   What Created the Forms? 29
   We Are Not Small And Powerless 34
   Oneness Holds Us to a Higher Standard 36
   Transhumanism 40

CH III NATURE'S LAWS OF CREATION 45
   Creating From Wholeness vs Separation in Order to Know 45
   A Cause and Effect Reality 48
   Jumping Timelines 59
   Images from Elsewhere 62
   Our Wild Card—Who We Are 65

- Group Creation ... 67
- Make Time To Create For Humanity ... 70
- Stillness ... 71

CH IV THE PANDEMIC BEGAN ... 75
- It's No Time to be Alone ... 78
- How Could This Be? ... 80
- Mass Formation Psychosis ... 84
- A Community Forms ... 90
- Now What? ... 92

CH V FREEDOM FROM FEAR ... 95
- Miracles Need Freedom from Fear ... 95
- Fear Inoculation ... 99
- Courage ... 105

CH VI RETRACT OUR CONSENT ... 107
- Who are These Brazen Globalists? ... 107
- Chaos And False Flags ... 110
- Our Purpose Here On Earth ... 111
- Money, Banks and Investments ... 114
- What Future Are We Investing In? ... 116
- Reduce Our Online Data ... 117
- Use Cash ... 118
- Non-Compliance and Satyagraha ... 120

CH VII SINGULAR FOCUS ... 125
- Deborah's Visions of the Future ... 126
- Your Role ... 128
- Anastasia and Kin's Domains ... 131

CH VIII HUMANITY'S GREATEST OPPORTUNITY ... 135
- Hearts Break Open ... 139
- Ceremony ... 140

ACKNOWLEDGEMENTS 145

RAYS OF HOPE AND REASONS TO PREVAIL 149

APPENDIX OF RESOURCES 165
    Declaration of Ethics for Artificial Intelligence 165
    Jesus' Commentary on the Resurrection 169
    Purification and the Purification Space Definitions from
    Oracle Girl 170
    The Declaration of Independence 171
    The Great Reset in a Nutshell 175
    The Hippocratic Oath 177
    The Hopi Prophecy 179
    The Ten Points of the Nuremberg Code of Medical
    Experimentation Ethics 179

DOCUMENTARIES AND OTHER REFERENCE
MATERIALS 183

BIBLIOGRAPHY 187

ABOUT THE AUTHOR 191

Also by Hope Ives Mauran

Available in Print:

The Key to Love, A Teaching from The Beings Of Light for an Enlightened Reality on Earth (2016)

Being the Miracle of Love: Conversations With Jesus (2013)

Be The Second Coming: A Guidebook To The Embodiment Of The Christ Within: A Personal Journey, Our Collective Destiny (2012)

Where the Wisdom Lies: A message From Nature's Small Creatures (2006)

Available in eBook:
Be The Second Coming: A Guidebook To The Embodiment Of The Christ Within: A Personal Journey, Our Collective Destiny (2012)

Teaching Audio CD: written and recorded

Emotional Transformation: Learn to Speak the Language of Creation

DEDICATION

This book is dedicated to the Love within all of us, that it may pour forth into this world through these words, this story and our hands, to find its solid rooting in the rich soil of this good Earth.

* * * * * * * * * * * * * * *

If a statement is not cited it is from my own inner wisdom higher self, or my innate divine intelligence.

In the recounting of the pandemic, if there are un-cited statements, their original source is no longer available online. Some sources have been censored and are no longer available at this time.

Sarah, Karen, Sam and Rachel are pseudonyms, to protect their privacy.

* * * * * * * * * * * * * * *

OVERVIEW

This book is a call to awaken to the excitement and opportunities of these times of rising frequency on Earth. The creation of a New Earth is now possible. Our New Earth will be based in Love and asks of us to be caring stewards, creators and holders of the Light of Love. Deep inner and outer changes are happening now as a result of this rise in frequency and will help us to transition to a new more loving and positive way of living together. This book offers a roadmap to a new and beautiful future.

The positive future for humanity rests upon our understanding of who we are and why we are here. We are not just our bodies; we are infinite, eternal Consciousness masquerading as humans. *Love is our true nature and we are all connected. Who we think we are matters at every level of our lives.* We and our monolithic identity have been entrapped in our bodies and minds for generations, where we have been experiencing ourselves as disconnected from each other and from all of Nature. We have lost touch with the interconnectedness of all life, our Source Creator, our innate power and role as creators and the Field of Love that surrounds and supports all of creation.

We have become victims to the outer world, when in fact it is our internal guidance, intuition and our heart that we need to listen to and follow to navigate these times of transition. We are multidimensional beings of love, creativity and transformation. Our positive future hinges on our ability to know who we are as infinite eternal Consciousness beyond the body. Knowing who we are expands the playing field of Life from being our immediate local surroundings to all of creation. This knowing moves us from being spectators to leaders, creators and builders of the New Earth. We are all critically important to this delicate process of evolutionary transformation.

The Earth's frequency is rising and the density that has hidden our ability to know ourselves as infinite eternal Consciousness is diminishing. We are now at the end of a great cycle of time, Kali Yuga; a 5000 year cycle is ending (in this century). Sadhguru,[1] the Indian mystic explained that it takes 25,920 years for our Solar System to circle a larger star. "Whenever our solar system comes closer to this big star, all the creatures living in our system rise to greater possibilities" this is called Satya Yuga. "When our system moves away from this big star, creatures in our system come to the lowest level of possibility. We say this is Kali Yuga" and we are leaving this low-point now.[2] So this time on Earth is very hopeful. It is a *new dawn* in the largest sense.

The rise in Earth frequency is also reflected in the upward spikes in the Schumann Resonance—the measurement of the electromagnetic radiation resonating between the Earth's surface and the ionosphere.

> *"Every second, a multitude of pulses travel around the world in this unique, resonant chamber between Earth and the ionosphere, sending colluding signals to all microorganisms. These signals couple us to the Earth's magnetic field. Named after their discoverer, these Schumann Resonances (SR) drive the harmonizing pulse for life in our world."*
> —Eric Thompson[3]

---

[1] Sadhguru is the leader of the worldwide Isha Foundation, https://isha.sadhguru.org/en/wisdom/article/kali-yuga-end-lies-ahead

[2] We are leaving Kali Yuga and entering Tetra Yuga, which is the second best time that can happen in a cycle of Yugas.. . . . Its effect on humanity and all life is not conjecture; it is rooted in a deep understanding about what happens with the human mind in relation to the planet." It has to do with Ether and the electromagnetism systems of the Earth. https://isha.sadhguru.org/en/wisdom/article/kali-yuga-end-lies-ahead

[3] Schumann "Resonance' Today website. https://www.disclosurenews.it/schumann-resonance-today-update/, https://www.disclosurenews.it/

The Schumann Resonance has risen from 7.8 Hz in 1954 to 35 Hz and higher now. "You can think of this as the Earth's heartbeat."[4] It affects our behavior, our emotions and the natural world. A higher frequency carries more information and therefore we have the opportunity now to know more, see more, feel more, love more and become more of who we already are. It affects the electrical conductivity of the atmosphere and hence all of us.

This increase in the Schumann Resonance supports Sadhguru's declaration of greater possibilities for humanity. Our placement in the galaxy supports a more enlightened human society. This is very good news!

This book is also about Truth. Both practical and spiritual truth at the same time. Practical, in that it presents some very real but uncomfortable, global situations that some people might not want to know about. I didn't want to learn of these things either—no one did. But I urge us all to push through any discomfort and investigate these truths for ourselves. The situation on Earth today involves the tragic scenario of many people dying prematurely.[5] Understanding this difficult situation just might save your life or even save your soul.[6] I say "save your soul" because the possible transhuman effects down the road, could disconnect your body from your soul. It would be horrible to look back on the choices we are making today and say, "If only we had known," or have nothing to say when our children ask us, "What did you do to prevent this from happening?" This book chronicles some of what happened during and after the pandemic and what continues to happen currently.

---

schumann-resonance-charts/,
[4] Earth's Vibrations Are Higher Than Ever! Is Our Consciousness Also Rising in Frequency? an online essay. https://www.reddit.com/r/Retconned/comments/6fnqgl/earths_vibrations_are_higher_than_ever_is_our/?rdt=57149
[5] *Died Suddenly* https://rumble.com/v1wac7i-world-premier-died-suddenly.html Directed by Matthew Skow and Nicholas Stumphauzer.
[6] See Rudolph Steiner's quote on pg. 88 in Ch IV, and the World Economic Forum advisor's quote on Pg 82 in Ch IV.

In a million years I would never have imagined that there are forces in our world purposefully working to harm and separate us from each other and from our innate power. Forces of manipulation, coercion and control have been steadily encroaching into our lives already for hundreds, maybe even thousands of years, bringing Earth destruction, population reduction, manipulation and transhumanism as their overarching goals. All this represents the manifestations of Kali Yuga's final act, and humanity's extreme and downward journey into separation from our divine essence. It is my hope and understanding that these negative forces *will naturally dissipate as the Earth's frequency rises*. However, this plan of coercion and manipulation has the potential to take many human lives. This human exodus has already begun as many are tragically dying. The data confirms that "all-cause" deaths have increased 40% in the 18-49 year old range since 2021.[7]

This Global plan that the negative forces have in place, would radically change who we are (i.e. transhumanism) and the way we all live *by the year 2030*. The negative forces wish to control humanity's freedoms, our health, creativity, reproduction, population, and access to Nature and the outdoors. They also plan to control Earth's resources …. water, lands, minerals, animals … everything. The globalists have a great deal invested in our not knowing what they are doing, they have set up life situations to ensure we all stay asleep to their plans. Several documentaries, interviews and books listed in the Resources Section, Bibliography and footnotes, reveal their well organized hidden plan. Their plan is dangerous, devastating, world-destabilizing and heartbreaking.

If we are to survive Agenda 2030, (the plan) it requires us to wake up and learn what is happening behind the scenes around the world.

---

[7] *Died Suddenly* documentary (https://rumble.com/v1wac7i-world-premier-died-suddenly.html), directed by Matthew Skow and Nicholas Stumphauzer, shows long string-like materials that are pulled out of people's arteries in the embalming process. It doesn't matter what someone died of, all the dead bodies have this phenomenon occurring, something that the funeral directors interviewed have never seen before.

We can move in a direction that will bring freedom, harmony, beauty and love to planet Earth. Once we know what is happening, it would be best to make clear choices and move forward to create a beautiful abundant reality that serves us all. We humans are powerful, resourceful, intelligent and plentiful enough to do this, when we join together. This is our chance to learn and know, make a clear choice and move forward to create the future we want to live within.

Like a cell divides, two Earths of different frequencies are splitting apart. There are two Earths now. The old one that is being encroached upon by controlling negative forces . . . and a new higher frequency Earth, that is being birthed and created now. The higher frequency Earth is forming in partnership with our inner shift to reclaim our interconnected and Love-based identity as Consciousness. We are creating it in partnership with the energy shifts happening as the Yuga cycles transition. These evolutionary changes will *naturally bring* Love-based New World societies that live in harmony, self-responsibility and in alignment with Nature. It is my understanding that the old Earth will run its course and eventually disappear.

This book navigates our internal and external transition to the New Earth. It coaches our *extrication* from the old Earth and guides our energetic and physical *creation* of the New Earth. There is no one-size-fits-all solution to how we will navigate this transition. There is however *one skill that we all must master, and that is the skill of staying focused upon what it is we* do *want*.

Inspiration and ideas for creating our collective future on the New Earth are offered here in expansive and general enough terms that most humans can support them, participate and contribute. We can seed the New Earth's creation with specific words, intention, spontaneous action and love, and Nature can help us to fill in the details. Our words and thoughts are that powerful!

It is a potent and very exciting time to be on Earth. Embodying love, uncovering truth and figuring out what's important in this world is

I called Karen to get Sarah's number so that I could deliver her package. There was a big snow storm brewing, with heavy winds and cold temperatures predicted. As I spoke to Sarah, she was heading into town to stock up on groceries and would try to stop by to pick up her package on my porch on the way back. She never made it to my house and the box sat out on the porch as the storm dropped its heavy load of snow, toppled trees and power lines for another day and a half. I had no telephone or internet, and the power was out, but I did at least have heat.

As the storm cleared, I decided to take the package over. I found a huge tree and electrical lines down across the road. The next day I finally made it through. In the frigid back hall amidst boots and coats I met Sarah—a natural beauty in a snug gray sweatshirt that couldn't hide her full belly. She was teary, alone, cold, and the house was slowly beginning to freeze. She was feeling overwhelmed and distraught. I offered that she could come stay at my house while the power was out. She said she had stocked up on food and wanted to stay there at Karen's.

Our meeting at that moment in time was perfectly choreographed. It eased some of her isolation in that moment, and in some small way made a big difference. I left, carrying her situation with me, and also I was reassured by seeing her trust in the natural process of birth. Her body knew what to do and she was sure of it. It inspired me to greater trust in myself and the world of Nature we live in.

What are the odds of her package arriving on my porch three miles away? Pretty low, I think. (Thanks FedEx or UPS!) It was a beautiful synchronicity that brought two strangers together in a moment of grace in that back-hall meeting that comforted us both.

Why is this story relevant? Sarah's story reminds me to trust that Love is all around us and connects the material world and all of us together outside of time. Love is scripting the future based on our spoken and unspoken wishes, hopes, prayers, intentions, dreams—and

---

process. https://en.wikipedia.org/wiki/Unassisted_childbirth

also based on our fears, our unconscious repetitive thoughts and behaviors. There is a greater hand, a natural order, that guides and holds us and brings to our experience what we imagine, create and attract. I sometimes call the Universe "the great sorter in the sky." It sends packages to the wrong house in order to connect people that will find joy and peace together. It's not actually outside of us or separate from us; it is who we all are in the largest sense.

> Have faith. Trust that you, your body and your mind are up to the task at hand.

This is a loving world that we can influence and work with individually and as a whole human family. How amazing and incredible is that! Synchronicities and miracles are everywhere waiting for us to join in the flow of their expression. Have you had similar kinds of synchronicities? A friend of mine keeps a journal of them because it can be so uplifting to remember these wonderful occurrences that defy our traditional explanations and logic.

There is reason for hope at this challenging time and much to be grateful for as the frequency of the Earth is rising, and the consciousness of humanity is cracking open to reveal more awareness, insight and Love. The miracles of this world are actually just demonstrations of the *higher order reality* that we all live within. The orchestration of miracles occurs within us, not outside of us. Trusting Love as the substrate of existence, as *"the healing force within and around all life,"*[10] has been easy to forget recently, having just come out of the uncertainty and heaviness of the pandemic. It's a relief to finally feel some freedom and ease returning to daily interactions, as the lightness that engenders synchronicities and miracles has returned. It's easier to remember this benevolent field when I take a moment to stop, become still and just notice it. Can you feel the Field of Love around you? For me it feels like gentle caressing coming

---

[10] From the quote at the top of Chapter I, received from Jesus directly by the author.

in from all sides. When I remember to notice it, it feels like having a friend everywhere I am.

The Field of Love

A Field exists only as a function.[11] It can't be seen. It is known by its effect and by our looking for it. That we exist in a "Field of Love" may sound like an airy-fairy spiritual idea, but Science substantiates a connecting Field[12] that is a medium for healing. In Marc Newkirk's,[13] talk entitled "Scientific Evidence of Metaphysical Truth,"[14] he profiled several scientists with impressive credentials from respected universities, and shared their research and findings that demonstrate our Oneness and the Field that connects us all. He said that new discoveries are happening so fast that most of us are not aware of the leading edge of science, energy and technology.

Remote healing is a perfect example of how we are all connected. For example, Marc's friend, Ji Xing Li, a Chigung Master,[15] can heal and rejuvenate cells from a distance. He was able to destroy cancer cells in a

---

[11] Joseph Chilton Pearce, (2002), *The Biology of Transcendence*, Park Street Press, Rochester VT, pg 84.

[12] Marc Newkirk, was a materials engineer, scientist, and inventor with his name on over 900 patents and an elected member of the National Academy of Engineering. In his talk entitled "Scientific Evidence of Metaphysical Truth' he shared research and findings that demonstrate our Oneness and the Field that connects us all. He also listed the 5 other traditionally known fields: Gravitational, electrical, magnetic, strong and the weak nuclear attraction fields.

[13] Marc Newkirk, with a team of intuitives, received the design from a higher dimension for the Lightfield, which is a coherent field environment they then built in Chester Massachusetts, with the intention of raising human consciousness. It is available for use by the public, in person or remotely. His talk "Scientific Evidence of Metaphysical Truth" is available at, https://www.conscioustechnologiesllc.com

[14] Available on the https://www.conscioustechnologiesllc.com/resources website, belonging to his son Ross Newkirk.

[15] Ji Xing Li, has outlined the studies done at the University of Pennsylvania in 2007 on this website. His book is also listed. https://www.naturalhealingcenter.com/creative/jixingli.htm

laboratory from 1700 miles away. He also rejuvenated a fifty-plus year old woman, changing her to being biologically twenty years younger. She even got her menstrual cycle back. Marc called him right after an explosion burned Marc's face and arm very badly, and he was in excruciating pain. Ji Xing Li was about to get on an airplane and so once he was in the air, he was able to work on Marc remotely. Marc described the feeling of Ji Xing Li work on him, and at one point the pain instantly disappeared. Marc's face showed no signs of scarring or disfigurement. Remote healing is a well documented phenomenon. It uses the Field of Love and Consciousness to reach out and connect from any distance or location. It is evidence that who we are is everywhere and thus we are able to influence whatever we focus upon. I think of it as non-local Love.

Love is not an add-on or an extra. It is the central theme, power and substance behind life. Love can *heal,* as Ji Xing Li demonstrated. Love can also *protect* as the following story illustrates.

Ben and the Gang

My friend Ben lived on the lower east side of Manhattan in the 1960's when there were gangs that targeted the hippies with violence, because the hippies were encroaching[16] into the gang's neighborhood. One night he was walking home late and was approached by a menacing gang of fifteen teenagers, who walked towards him, each one with a weapon in their hand, because he was a hippie and had long hair. They wanted to attack him and "bring him down" as Ben described it. They blocked his escape and he had to back up. There was a small building ten feet behind him, and as they steadily approached him, he slowly backed up against it. Ben said, "Hey what are you doing?" He couldn't imagine why anyone would want to hurt him, because he had a heart full of Love.

---

[16] The hippies were "yuppifying" the neighborhood (1960's style), which meant the local families couldn't afford the rents that the hippies were willing and able to pay. They had asked the hippies to stay away, and this is why the gang threatened Ben in this way.

When his back hit the wall, one of the gang said, "He's okay." The gang parted and Ben walked forward right through them and on out. I asked him if he shook afterwards as he walked home, and he said, "When you are filled with the power of Love, you don't shake."

Standing within Love, embodying it like Ben did, our world is a benevolent place. Love responds with and for our thoughts and actions, crafting the miracle of the parting of the sea of young men. Love is the reigning field of energy here on Earth, and it is ours to *embody* as well.

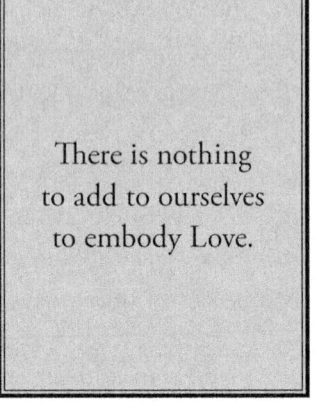

There is nothing to add to ourselves to embody Love.

As embodied Love, we have walked through a doorway of sorts. We have ascended in the time at hand, essentially to a New Earth environment of our own making. We have proverbially walked off the cliff onto the Bridge of Light that is there by our allowing our inherent Love and Light to shine forth. And ironically, it is done not by additions to who we are, but subtraction of who we are not!

We are not limited, even though resources on Earth appear to be. We are not lost to the Love that is within and around us; we are simply blind to it, and have learned another language that overwrites it. We are not who and what we have been taught. We are so much more. And so, if we were all awakened to this, there would be no problem that could not be solved. The way that this creation of the New Earth is to be unfolded depends on all of us. As we see more of the human potential and we practice our loving actions of togetherness, offering and sharing—and counter our ego's formulaic patterns of self-centeredness—we can lift the systems of Life to the next level.

Love also helps to make possible the *correction* of anything, as this next story illustrates.

Ross' Grace

My friend Ross Newkirk had a firewood business in high school, where he routinely handled chainsaws, a powerful gas fueled log splitter and other large machinery. One Sunday morning, his father offered to help him split wood before they went to church. They worked rhythmically together; his Dad put the logs on the splitter while Ross handled the control and then they switched. They got into a rhythm again, Ross put the log in place, Marc activated the control lever, and the hydraulic arm powerfully pushed the log into the knife edge and it split the log in two. That morning was remarkable in Ross' memory. When he got up that morning and looked out the window of his bedroom at the oak tree outside, the birds were chirping, the sun was shining, there was something very special about the day. They were working at great speed—set the log, activate the control lever, crunch, split, remove… and repeat. The firewood pile got bigger. Ross grabbed the next log with his left hand at the butt end of the log, not along the sides as he had done before, and his Dad activated the control. Ross screamed, his Dad reversed the control. Ross lifted his hand and one finger of the glove fell to the ground. Two other fingers of the glove were partially severed. He could feel an overwhelming, surreal, out-of-body sensation. He looked at his Dad as he removed the rest of the glove and found that all his fingers were there, whole and intact. His father said, "*I would have given my life for your fingers.*" Ross feels certain that those words, their deep shared Love for each other, and the elicited Grace in that moment saved his fingers. They were both so touched, they hugged each other, both feeling that something really big had just happened. They went inside to share the story with Ross' mother.

Ross's glove.

As Ross explained years later, "It was a hugely remarkable experience. My Dad and I talked about Grace a lot after that. There is this Love from the Universe and when we do our best, it looks out for us, We can trust that. When I doubt things in life, I put on that glove that I saved all these years, and I remember that positive Love and act of Grace. In a human sense, I made a mistake and an act of Grace went way beyond it." Ross continued, "We can reach for big things, even when we put our foot out there and don't see something to stand on, we can still be supported."

Creating a New Earth is an extraordinarily huge event, and we can have faith that we will be supported in this great task, just as Ben and Ross were in their moments of need.

> Your best is good enough.- Marc Newkirk

Trusting that higher level of Grace and Loving support is what we have the chance to do now. It requires a singular focus upon what it is that we do want to create, see and experience in our world. It is not something that can be created otherwise. Our potency as Creators is very concentrated and part of our innate human nature. There is a way in going forward that allows our highest visions to become reality, and in using the Laws of Nature, we give the Earth the chance to shine. And so the Consciousness that we all are—aligned with Love, and in use of the Laws of Creation—shines a bright Light into the future to illuminate the New Earth into being.

What do you see when you imagine a positive future for yourself, your community and the world?

More Evidence for The Field of Love

The rising energy frequency of the Earth empowers us to greater heights of awareness and sensitivity. The Field of Love can be felt by our bodies as energy. For years I have been aware of how my body is spontaneously guided to put my hand in a certain position in response to something I feel in the energy environment around me. It's like my body has a mind of its own. It happened for the first time when I was driving on a winding road with my son, and I made the gesture with my hand with open slightly bent fingers and just held it. I didn't know why, but I was impelled from within to do it. As we rounded the next corner, there was a car off the road. An accident had occurred. I realized that I had made the hand position to assist in raising the energy of the area and for the people involved, soothing the stress of the accident, the fear, the adrenaline and harmonizing the field that connects us all.

It has happened many times since then. Sometimes I know why, sometimes it is a mystery, I just do it. Occasionally it happens when someone is speaking as a victim, or projecting their anger or imagining an undesirable outcome.

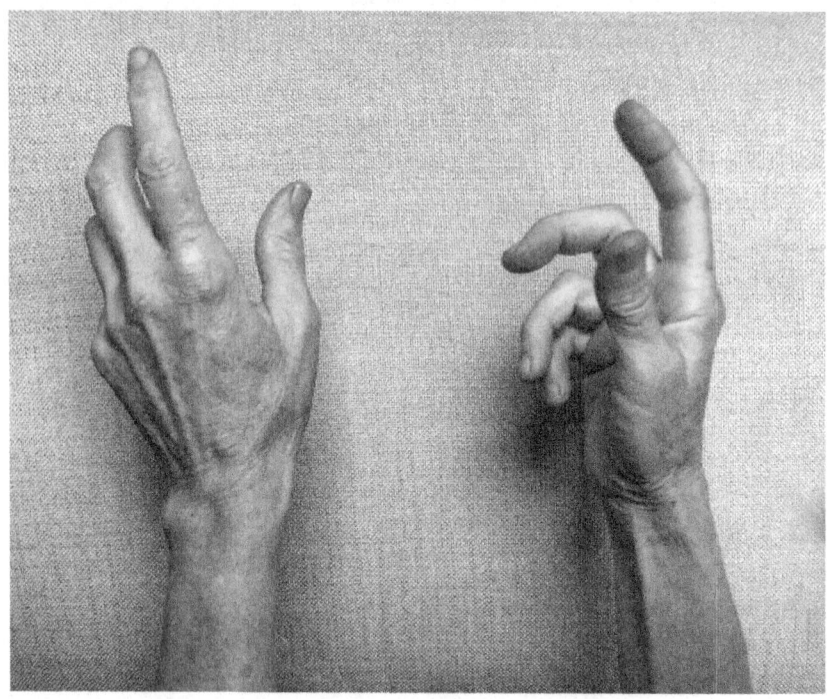

The hand position that modifies the energy in the surrounding area.

One time I was near Denver, Colorado with my son. We had parked and were walking down a steep embankment toward a trail that goes alongside a creek meandering along the valley floor. I found myself doing the hand position aimed towards the ground. Then we walked for an hour or so, enjoyed the creek and the many families passing by and returned the same way. As we approached the same place, my impulse to do it returned. (I had forgotten that I did the hand position before in this same spot.) My (patient) son and I just stood still as I did it again for several minutes. I wondered why, and the thought that an ambush happened there at some time in the past came to me. So perhaps I was clearing the old energy imprint of violence in that location.

I later discovered that the hand position is a position that has classically been used by many saints, sages, wise women and healers for millennia. **It is a frequency adjuster.** Positioning the hand and fingers in this way is an alignment with a higher frequency band of Light energy. It's like swimming underwater at Earth's lower frequency and having a snorkel to breathe at a higher frequency. It is reaching to the higher order of love and harmony, and bringing a healing balm of Light energy into the surrounding area for about three hundred feet.

It is not uncommon for the hand position to be done by babies and children who are still able to feel beyond this realm to the higher realms above the dense frequency of Earth. This attuning serves at a deep level to heal the one doing it, as well as the land and other people within the vicinity. That is why it was done at the accident site that first time. There are in fact many ways to tap into and harmonize the energy at hand and many of the healing arts and sciences do this, either on purpose, or accidentally. I discovered recently that there are paintings of Jesus demonstrating this same hand position, one by Leonardo Da Vinci, sold for $450 million dollars in 2017.[17] I wonder if that price was for the priceless and potent hand position?

It is also a powerful opportunity to reset the frequency of people, animals and the Earth on all levels around a location. Raising the energy

---

[17] https://www.npr.org/sections/thetwo-way/2017/11/16/564527819/da-vinci-portrait-of-christ-sells-for-record-shattering-450-million

to a higher harmonic of what is occurring can enhance cognition and raise consciousness. As the frequency is lifted and harmonized, the Earth's energy becomes less like a collapsed structure and repairs itself allowing more light through as it is restored to its proper structural pattern. Imagine a framework of balls and sticks forming a cube, like in a children's a tinker toy construction set.

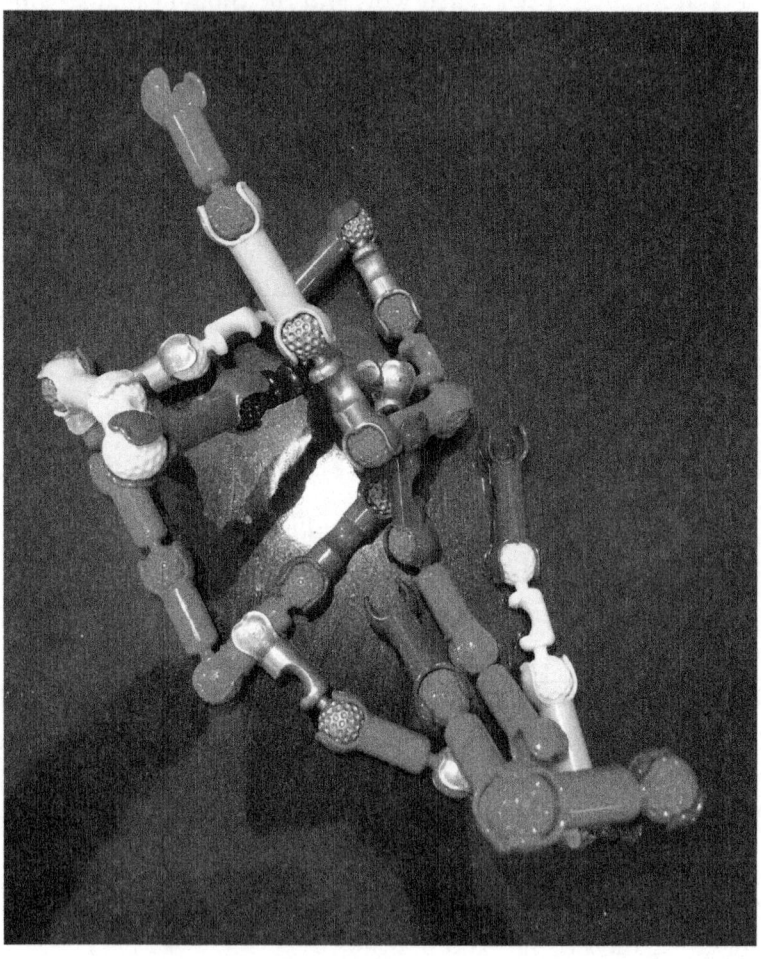

If the energetic structure is twisted and pulled and collapses, it is denser and blocks the light.

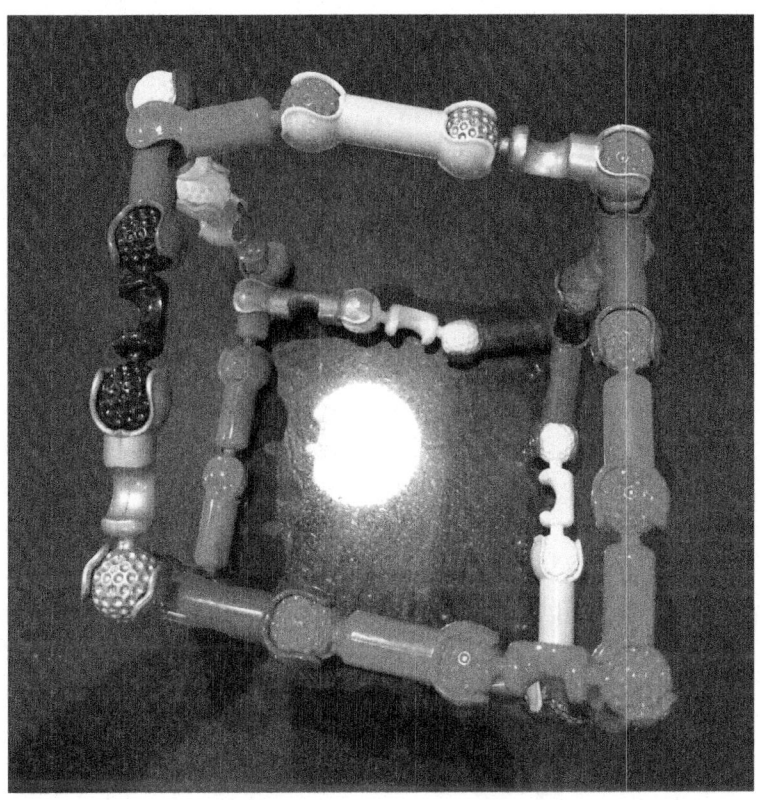

As the structure is put back upright into place,
the Light can flow to and through it.

The chaos is removed, by restoring the energetic structure of the field that exists in a space. Whether distortions are from an historic event, or the current situation unfolding in the present, it matters not. They can all be influenced to heal. And so, when there is more Light that can penetrate into a location, there is more Love, more peace, more relaxation and ease that results. The hand position can do this.

Anyone can do this. It just requires willingness to respond to the impulse because it can be inconvenient or socially awkward. There is a choreography that our higher self within us would follow if we allowed it to more often. It includes happiness, joy, compassion, sharing, love and more such impulses. It is a sad commentary that this impulse is either not allowed or is trained out of some young children through various practices, and also the new devices (like television and cell phones), that like vampires are sucking the energy and light from humanity, dimming their inner light and stealing their energy. We are all desperately in need of this life energy in order to create the beautiful life and world that we came here to create.

> Notice and act upon the loving and harmonizing impulses that flit through your mind.

This hand position and other kinds of energy transformation can be done very simply by noticing impulses and thoughts suggesting a physical movement, hand position or the tiny inner impulses of generosity. Even as simple as the urge to pick up the phone to call someone. Like a small waft of smoke, the impulse dissipates quickly, and if one gets in the habit of noticing such impulses of Love, generosity, healing and goodness, and follows through, like breaching a dam, the energy gets more powerful and the impulses become stronger and clearer. It is in this way that we can transform our relationship with the Field that connects all life on Earth. Holding the intention to be in service to the Field of Love and Light between us all is one way to convey this inner intention to all levels of our human personality. Getting our personality on board at all levels is an important alignment that opens up vast potentials and opportunities to bring healing to the world.

I've noticed that sometimes this connection kicks in when I have an uncomfortable thought. My discomfort interrupts the trajectory of my familiar path, like a bump jostles me in a car. I am bumped out of the groove up to another level of energy that serves a higher good and connects at a higher energetic level.

By cultivating the perspective of ourselves that is outside of the physical hierarchy, we can transcend the laws of this physical world. We are capable of far more than we currently know.

We have even been distracted from investigating what we can do, as we are inundated with work, tasks, distractions and information daily, keeping us occupied with the surface level of engagement with life. If you have the impulse to do something with your body (and are willing to look a bit strange) or speak some loving blessing, declaration or prayer out loud, do it! The energy of Creation is fast, focused and lovingly fierce. I command things to occur or not occur, reformulating mis-creations. The impulse to create with loving intention is compelling in that I *must* do it; (and there is no reason not to do it) it is a choiceless choice. Words come with the Light of Truth and a clarity that is from another level of my being. I feel purified, energized and activated afterwards. Loving actions from our higher self fill us with joy.

Simply being aware of the energy impulse to do something, and trying it, is a start. My friend Veronica feels the energy coming from her hands and can actually see it in beams of Light from her fingertips in the dark. I too saw light come from my hand in the middle of the night once while I was energy healing my infant son when he was sick. We are all filled with light, and thus seeing it should not be such a surprise to us anymore! Healing with our hands is possible and common with energy healers and medical intuitives, who can even see inside the body. Our hands emit energy as seen or unseen light, and can help to heal. If it pops into your mind, use your healing energy the next time someone is in pain or sick. Consciousness is everywhere and responds to itself. Our focus directs and qualifies the light energy we posses.

A Light In the Head

Humans are truly beings of Light. In the article *Is DNA the Next Internet?* Dan Eden examines some amazing claims made by Russian scientists.[18] It describes how light, or photons of light, are the mechanism

---

[18] *Is DNA the Next Internet?* Dan Eden examines some amazing claims made by Russian scientists. Link extends to next page: https://www.esalq.usp.br/lepse/imgs/conteudo_thumb/Are-humans-really-beings-of-light.pdf. Interestingly by measuring the photon emission and frequency of a substance, its cancer-causing

for communication inter- and intra-cellularly. The photons (or units) of light help the parts within a cell that need to interact or communicate, to find each other. Light also drives communication within the body's nervous system, within groups of the same species *and* between species. Light is far more important and prevalent to our biological functioning than we have been aware of.

There is another frontier in understanding light, where a Light goes on inside our heads. This gentle shining light can come in meditation, or while in nature. A Light turns on and the eyes see a golden brightness when both closed and open. If our eyes are closed we think someone turned on a light in the room, it lingers for a few minutes and then disappears. This Light seemingly shines when one is being neutral, empty of thoughts and at peace. It comes rarely and unpredictably, and evidently it occurs through the Pineal Gland. The Pineal Gland is an ancient eye of sorts. It is the physical part of an energetic phenomenon of the "all seeing eye," or the "third eye." Manly Hall[19] calls the "Eye of God."

Oracle Girl's definition[20] sheds light on this: "Pineal Gland: Contains the matrix of all life and possesses light bearing capacity. Controls the transmission of our body signal out into the Universe. Processes and regulates internal luminescence and the swell of instructions from our Pituitary Gland."

The Pineal Gland plays an important role in the transmission of Light throughout the body. The Light within us is a means of communication within our bodies and between levels of ourself. Could this Light in the head be our eternal Light, our Divine essence entering unimpeded into

---

status or its toxicity can be predicted by the substance's ability to scramble light signals used in the body for communication, cell regulation and a multitude of other processes. https://www.wakingtimes.com/is-dna-the-next-internet/

[19] Hall, Manly, (2015), the Pineal Gland: the Eye of God, comprising Chapter XVI of Manly Hall's Man: The Grand Symbol of the Mysteries, Marshfield Center, CT, Martino Publishing, pg 5.

[20] Www.oraclegirl.org, glossary

this dimensional reality as the Light within our heads? Light is a Universal language: it needs no translation. In high frequency states, where people are connecting to higher dimensions, their physicality becomes less solid. People have disappeared into just an outline of Light in photographs taken of them, or into just a line of chakras (energy centers) aligned up the center of their body with no body outline evident.

The Light in the head is like a halo, as Jesus is often depicted with. It is an indicator of alignment with the Truth of Love. It is healing, in and of itself. As we go further into the higher frequency zone in the galaxy the entire planet has the potential opportunity for this level of physical demonstration. It cannot be acquired—it is simply present in the right/correct circumstances. A frequency attractor is how you might describe its essential origin.

> Hold your frequency as *one with all life*, as naturally as a bird flies across the blue sky.

As this higher "normal" is anchored in more and more beings on Earth, a quantum shift in how the physical reality is seen and interacted with occurs. Like shifting upward in an old standard transmission sports car, life moves forward at a faster higher frequency from the Presence of beings present on Earth that anchor and stabilize the Field of Love and Light that the Earth exists within. There is much greatness that lies latent in the human family. We currently only use a fraction of our brain capacity. Catalyzing this kind of release of an old way of being is what these higher frequency times, clear choices and a vision of a more loving Earth environment will bring. One Light catalyzes another's as we create Love's New Earth together. Aligning with the truth of Love and Oneness helps our world as much as it helps us.

Years ago, as I was finishing this painting of a tree that has people in the crown and walking in a long line on the ground, my guidance was to put a halo around all the people in it. At the time, I was astonished to be told that *all of the people* in the painting were to have the halo of what I call Christ light, or Unconditional Love. What an amazing time we live in on Earth when this is becoming possible.

Even though there is much variety in the human form and ways of thought, this inner Light can help us navigate the path towards a Golden Age on Earth. We humans move forward in our world, literally by referencing the outer world and by noticing the opportunities that come to us physically.

What if there were another way to navigate this world? What if the way forward was shown by the inner Light? By an actual inner Light, enlightening the path ahead? This is possible as more and more of us hold the higher frequencies of Light energy that are showering upon the Earth. It is being infused into the land, the water, the animals, the plants—and us humans. One way we can capture this light potential is to sit very, very still and just *feel* our bodies. A daily practice of doing this can bring this possibility closer. The divine light shining through our physical forms is the evidence of our soul's journey from separation to knowing our Oneness.

Why do you think that the negative forces that wish for an alternative future and to control humanity are changing the energies throughout all the Earth? It is to thwart this natural opportunity at this time of reclaiming our True selves upon this Earth. What the global plan is doing is like having a mirror set across the finish line: as the populace is racing towards an end point for manifest reality. The mirror creates confusion and chaos. This is what is occurring now on Earth with the radiation of the antennae[21] across the world and the satellites in the lower atmosphere. They are attempting to disturb our natural energy fields. It is with this realization that we can transcend this interference by simply realizing it has NO HOLD upon us. It has no force within it that can truly touch who we are. Its emanations are simply *coercive*, and if our frequency is above that level, there is no way it can harm or interfere with us or our capacity to hold the Light that is available now on Earth.

---

[21] Reference to 5G, and its thousands of satellites in the lower atmosphere. This website of Americans for Responsible Technology offers many resources for supporting local control of 5G installations. https://www.americansforresponsibletech.org/ This Federal Communications Commission website, https://www.fcc.gov/5G, illustrates their desire to override local control of installations. Demonstrating their valuing of speed over health and safety. Chairwoman Rosenworcel has said, "if we want broad economic growth and widespread mobile opportunity, we need to avoid unnecessary delays in the state and local approval process. That's because they can slow deployment." See the website wirelesseducation.org for resources to support a healthy future in the wireless age we are in.

And so, as we work to entrust ourselves to this process of changing with the rising frequency on Earth, our *willingness* and *holiness* must interact, as we realize that all that is possible is already here, awaiting our notice, our choice and our willingness to be true to ourselves at our highest and truest level. Now it is a time to use the emanations of Light for far greater plans and paths. We are on the precipice of a grand opportunity where the fullness of who we are is revealed to us—en mass[22]—with many, many awakening to this higher potential and opportunity to dwell *within* and *as* the Light of Love … God/Source/Creator. This "Light in the head" emanation is an opportunity that is looming for all mankind. Do not be dissuaded from acting as an individual, simply tend to business and hold your frequency as One with all Life, as naturally as a bird flies across the blue sky. Naturally, with ease, the Light within begins to shine. It is not of itself a goal; it is simply a reminder of this Self that we are beyond the body, awaiting its time on Earth in its fullest expression in our life and body. Love heals and flows as this is manifest.

A Mass Awakening

This grand opportunity could take the form of a mass awakening. What might such an awakening look like? I recall a late morning in New York City when I was walking up the stairs out of the subway, and something lifted from me as all the people became exquisitely beautiful. I felt so much love for everything and everyone in the crowd around me. It lasted but a few minutes and then it was gone. I didn't do anything to make that happen, although I was happy and feeling love in my heart in that moment. If this same "lifting" was lifted from all humans, this world would change overnight. It was a glimpse of what form a possible mass awakening could take.

---

[22] Nancy Rebecca said the same thing in her Interview of Pam Gregory, an Astrologer and Nancy Rebecca, speaking about a surge of blue light that will bring mass awakening to humanity. https://www.youtube.com/watch?v=eHnWD7eiGRg

This potent time on Earth supports the Light going on within and around us all. Our full multidimensional self—all parts of ourselves that exist inside of this physical Earth and beyond this density in other dimensions—become more evident because our higher frequency opens the door to our own full presence. We become immune to the coercion and controlling energies as we recognize them for what they are: lower frequency, less powerful and sourced in fear. They need not affect us. It is a choice we can make with our focus, intent and alignment with Nature, with Love and with our Source.

Non forgiveness, of ourselves or others holds us outside of this Light potential and keeps us from this higher level expression of Light. Our opportunity now in this transition time is to heal the [mis]understanding and belief that we are separate, that has kept us from our power as Light, as Love and to live in harmony with the whole of Life and Nature. We have generations of trauma that we can't move beyond without some help. In operating solely from the level of what we see and feel physically, we are locked into this downward spiral of human life. Forgiveness is powerful and this knowledge of who we truly are, who everyone else is, of our inner Light and our Oneness, in this rising frequency environment, gives us this chance to hit a reset button and start again. Too bad there aren't yet any glasses that can show us the true divine essence of everyone we see. It would make this important transformation easy. Which it is not!

How do we forgive ourselves and others? If we can define *Forgiveness* as simply the awareness that nothing that has been done to us or on Earth is actually True—because we aren't actually these bodies and these beings we think we are—we can forgive anything and everything as not actually having happened. Or we can realize that our grief and our gripes aren't worth holding onto in the face of this higher opportunity presenting itself. In full and *complete* Forgiveness of the world there is nothing that stands in the way of our True expression and the "full monte" of miracle potentials. This must be imprinted in our awareness of the landscape ahead. These are unique and wonderful times.

The only thing that sets us apart from the possibility of miracles in our expression and experience is non-forgiveness. In the simplest of terms, forgiveness consists of being kind. Be kind to yourself, allow yourself errors—and correct them. Allow others' errors and be patient in your awareness that they are not the seeming human (fallible and imperfect), they are One with the Creator God and nothing that occurs at this level in the human body changes that Truth. WE are all ONE with the Creator/Source/God. As brothers and sisters of the Light we can allow ourselves to Love no matter what, by seeing through the physical to that which is before all this world, to that which joins us all as One. It has magnificent qualities that transform all Life around us, making possible and evident the miracles that are within and around us all.

So much is possible for us now. In union with our divine origin, miracles as extreme as raising the dead are possible.[23] So, this knowledge of *who we are* prior to the manifest world, puts us above or before its physical Laws. Transcendence is possible with this knowledge and transfers to our bodies and world. It's another "higher" opportunity which is here now for us all to discover. In the manifest reality or the physical world there is a hierarchy, which is not true at the level of our identity as Consciousness. Consciousness is not influenced at this level of physical form, it is just at the level of the body and world that a hierarchy apparently exists. Understanding this difference helps us to realize that there is no order of difficulty at the level of Consciousness. Consciousness can think of anything large or small, without limitation, and thus assist in its creation.

---

[23] From one of Marc Newkirk's 's talks entitled "The Astounding Convergence of Physics and Metaphysics," *part 3 of 4 in the series*, at the 50 minute mark. he shared a story of Madame Sun Chulin, a Chigung Master, from Chinese Geology University, Beijing, who sprouted denatured seeds by human intention, in minutes, with hundreds of successful trials. Some of the peanuts she sprouted had been boiled or microwaved. He said "she could raise the dead." When asked if she could raise the dead she recounted bringing a rabbit to life as a child, and at a state dinner bringing a cooked shrimp on the table to life, so that it was running around on the table. Available from https://www.conscioustechnologiesllc.com/resources

Trusting in the Field of Love and Forgiveness (with a capital "F")[24] can help us live in peace *and* bring peace to this world.

> *Peacemaking doesn't mean passivity. It is the act of interrupting injustice without mirroring injustice, the act of disarming evil without destroying the evildoer, the act of finding a third way that is neither fight nor flight but the careful, arduous pursuit of reconciliation and justice. It is about a revolution of love that is big enough to set both the oppressed and the oppressors free.*
>
> —Shane Claiborne[25]

"A revolution of Love" is inevitable when we feel the support of the Field of Love that surrounds us, and know who we Truly Are. This Love, with a capital L, is the Love that can find its way to Forgiveness with a capital F, and the Forgiveness of our parents, our teachers, our trauma, all victimhood and violence and all that has held us apart from our True nature as Love embodied on Earth. What would a revolution of Love look like for you in your life and in your community?

---

[24] Forgiveness with a capital F is in contrast to forgiveness that makes others wrong and then benevolently forgives them, Forgiveness is of a higher order.

[25] Shane Claiborne, from *Common Prayer: A Liturgy for Ordinary Radicals*.

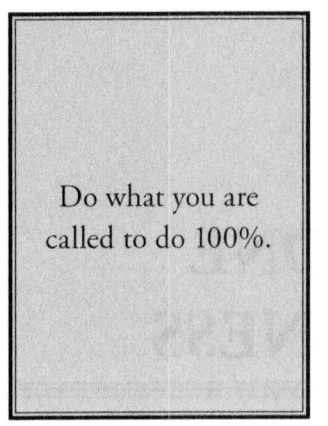

Do what you are called to do 100%.

Sam reached out to the man *as a brother with Love.* Sam himself knew instinctively that everyone on that subway was connected, that there was a bond that could be called forth to bring the man back into the family of humanity.

When we know who we *Truly Are* (beyond the body), we realize that we and the world are indivisible. We know everyone as our brother or sister. We know all life forms as part of our family. The Lakota phrase "Mitakuye oyasin" is a greeting that means "All My Relations." It is used in Lakota Native American Ceremonies to greet the animals, plants and all life. On the spiritual path, many understand that we are *all One* in some way. "The spirit that moves through all things"[26] is another name used for it. How is it possible that we are related to all life? Until I came upon Vedanta, I was a bit fuzzy on how this Unity-of-all-things worked. Vedanta[27] is a "means of knowledge," for knowing our True identity. It's a time-tested, effective explanation of how we can discover for ourselves that we are all Consciousness, and how Consciousness relates to our human bodies and the physical world. It's a challenging understanding because its not physically possible to know who we are with our five senses and our brain, because there is nothing outside of us as Consciousness and thus from our bodies we are unable to see or sense who we Truly are, which is Consciousness.

Having an explanation of how we are joined and All One is a solid foundation for moving into a higher order relationship with ourselves, each other, with Forgiveness and with the Earth. It may be that with the rise in Schumann Resonance now, and the movement into the higher

---

[26] This is a phrase that Tom Brown, Jr. uses often in his teachings of the ways of Nature at the Tracker School in New Jersey.

[27] Vedanta is an ancient means of understanding life and who we truly are, originating in India thousands of years ago.

possibilities of Tetra Yuga, we can all know who we are more easily than was possible in the greater density of the past.

Who Are We?

I draw upon Vedanta with deep gratitude to the teachers[28] who have shared this knowledge. Its oral tradition has been passed down for millennia. As Vedanta explains, we often view ourselves as our name and our role in life—mother, father, daughter, son, teacher. Over time one identity label dissolves into another. They are all the same, in that they are all:

mortal,
limited,
separate,
changeable,
unique,
concerned and
doers.

These labels are not who we are.

In fact we are actually Non-dual Consciousness /Awareness, which is:

limitless,
unborn,
whole,
complete,
eternal,
action-less and
unconcerned.

---

[28] James Schwartz, Swami Svatmananda, Swami Paramarthananda and Swami Dyananda, their contact information is in the Rays of Hope and reasons to prevail, in the back of the book.

We are the Consciousness within and beyond, around and through all things. I think of it as the background field that holds everything including our bodies. All these physical things never touch us, don't hold us and can't harm us. There is nothing that is not Consciousness. There is nothing outside of us. All the many dimensions, densities and realities exist within non-dual Consciousness. Non-dual Consciousness is free of being influenced by everything physical that appears in it. All those physical things require subject/object relationships which are impossible in non-dual Consciousness. Non-dual Consciousness cannot be seen, touched, heard, felt, moved or contained because there is nothing that is not it, it is indivisible. It cannot be captured in any subject/object relationship. When we know how to acknowledge, interpret and navigate our *freedom to focus anywhere as Consciousness,* we can't be contained. For example, imagine somewhere far away, like the moon, the Eiffel Tower, or your childhood home, your Consciousness awakens to an image of that place, and your consciousness is there. Nothing can contain us as Consciousness. This is our freedom. In this way, we are released from the prison our body can sometimes be. (People who have had out of body experiences from near death experiences (NDE), or during surgery, float unseen above their bodies and see and hear what is being said by the doctors and nurses. They experience that their own body is not who they are.)

"I salute that consciousness in which all things abide, from which they emerge, which is all and everywhere and which is all in all and eternal; which is the purifier of all and whose vision is most meritorious."- Bhusunda the crow, a story in Vasistha'sYoga[29] by Swami Venkatesananda

This *most meritorious* vision of the world through the lens of Consciousness can transform the world. What we choose to see determines who we are.

The *"I"* sense in me and the *"I"* sense in you is also non-dual Consciousness. Perhaps this explains why so many psychic and

---

[29] Venkatesananda, Swami, (1993), *Vasistha'sYoga,* Albany, NY, State University of New York Press, pg 358.

metaphysical phenomenon (like mental telepathy, medical intuition and remote viewing) are possible. There is no separation between us. Consciousness is everywhere and connects us all. So, our "*I*" sense is not influenced or entrapped by matter, experiences, or the births and deaths of the material world. This knowledge changes how we see and value the material world.

To get a sense of what it means to be non-dual Consciousness appearing as a human body, Vedanta offers some comparisons:

> The essence of fire is heat
> The essence of sugar is sweetness
> The essence of the pot is clay
> The essence who we are is Consciousness / Awareness.

It is Consciousness that makes us who we are. Our *form* is human, but the essence of our content and quality is Consciousness. I love this quote from Vedanta teacher James Schwartz:

> *"You are free, your nature is love and you are beautiful.*
> *"Who you are is the source of all happiness and joy."*

Vedanta is a way to see through the physical world and position ourselves to jump off the wheel of reincarnation, freeing us from the entrapment of Earth and physicality when at the moment of "death" we know ourselves to be limitless Consciousness and not the failing body, our unresolved emotions, or absolutely anything else other than Consciousness!

What Created the Forms?

Vedanta explains that Consciousness did not create this world (Consciousness is action-less). Maya, an eternal principle within Consciousness, creates the manifest physical worlds.

"Maya is the delusory power inherent in the structure of creation, by which the One appears as many. Maya is the principle of relativity, inversion, contrast, duality, and oppositional states."[30]

Maya is like a mirror, Maya coagulates, solidifies or distorts pure Consciousness into all the things of the world. This quote explains what our body is, from esteemed Vedanta teacher Swami Paramarthananda.

> *This consciousness does not belong to the bodies. The bodies themselves function as a mirror. A mirror has no light of its own. If the mirror is kept under sunlight, the sunlight will reflect upon the mirror's surface and it will shine. By virtue of this reflected light, the mirror can illumine other things, not by its original light, but by its borrowed light. Thus the non-luminous becomes luminous. In a similar way, the insentient becomes sentient because of reflected consciousness. Each body has no life of its own, but is made sentient by the reflected light of consciousness.*
>
> *This all-pervading consciousness enlivens the entire universe. It is the reason the cosmos functions in an orderly manner, like a vast macrocosmic organism. Just as the cells and organs of our bodies function in a harmonious manner, so too does the universe. If we disturb this natural harmony, it offsets the balance and results in undesirable consequences. The universe is not a chaotic mass of inert matter. Pervaded and enlivened by pure consciousness, it functions intelligently.* [31]

---

[30] Definition of Maya, from a forgotten source, my apologies, it was on a slide from a talk I did in 2020 called "Who Am I *Really*?" Perhaps from James Swartz, Swami Paramarthananda or Swami Dyananda.

[31] Excerpt From *Vedanta: The Big Picture Swami Paramarthananda of Chennai*, written by Rory Mackay posted by James Schwartz on Face Book.

"We do not have many consciousnesses, we do not even have one consciousness, we have only consciousness." —*Swami Dayananda Saraswati*[32]

It's helpful to learn that Consciousness doesn't *create* the world and Consciousness doesn't *become* the world. Vedanta says Consciousness *appears as* the world. And thus, Consciousness makes no delineation between evil and good, either one is able to appear within it. Evil appears as a mis-creation or a distortion by humanity (and other mechanical life forms). Regardless of what is reflected in Maya's mirror, which shows us the manifest world, it has no capacity to harm who we truly are as non-dual Consciousness. And yet its compelling images and forms can keep us entranced and hypnotized, anchored to the five senses, our bodies, and alone without the knowledge of our true identity, and possibility for life.

The dots, represent Non-dual Consciousness, they are everywhere. Maya's influence upon Consciousness creates the cosmic egg—all physical form and densities and dimensions of reality, all within Consciousness. Consciousness is all there is in all you see.

---

[32] Swami Dyananda Saraswati, a revered Vedanta teacher who lead the Arsha Vidya Ashram in Saylorsburgh, PA.

This is the tiniest bit of Vedanta. I highly recommend its study. Vedanta is a means of knowledge for removing our life stream from the wheel of reincarnation. Perhaps these ancient Rishis, or holy ones, who received this wisdom knew of the simulation that David Icke identifies this world as, (in his book *The Dream*) and thus passed this Vedanta wisdom along as a way to escape the simulation's grip and the cycle of birth and death. If reincarnation is a manifestation of the 'simulation' and the denser energies of Kali Yuga, the great cycle of time that we are now leaving, then its days are numbered. Vedanta doesn't encourage the idea that we have the power to create. That is a leap I am taking as I go on, in the next chapter, to discuss the Laws of Creation—the Laws which apply to us as we navigate this physical world in our inert human bodies.

A Course In Miracles is rather unyielding on what the body is:

> *The body is the ego's idol; the belief in sin* [separation] *made flesh and then projected outward. This produces what seems to be a wall of flesh around the mind, keeping it prisoner in a tiny spot of space and time, beholden unto death, and given but an instant in which to sigh and grieve and die in honor of its master. And this unholy instant seems to be a life."*[33]

Our bodies were created to entrap us and enslave us. This, in rather depressing terms, points out how our identity as being "just the body" taints our life. Our way out of the trap that our body-identification can appear to be is through this *knowledge of who we are and what purpose we put upon the body*. Experiences of war, hatred and suffering originate from not knowing we are all connected. This is why this understanding of who we are helps in creation of a New Earth paradigm.

Our identity as Consciousness means that the world, the Universe, all the dimensions, densities and realities and thus all people, animals,

---

[33] *A Course in Miracles, Circle of Atonement edition, (2017), The Circle of Atonement, Inc.,* Ch 20, VI, 11:1-2.

insects, fungi, angels, fairies, devas, gods and devils, exist within us. We can communicate with other people, plants, animals, rocks, trees, the Earth and more. We humans are not victims; we are deeply embedded within the creation and designed as card-carrying creators, no different than the Creator of the Earth.

> "*Your information, memories, knowledge, skills, experiences, they are not held by your body. Your body is just a user interface between you and the physical universe.*"
> —*Earth Files* by Inelia Benz

This footnote in *A Course in Miracles, Circle of Atonement edition,*[34] pegs this delineation between who we are and our body.

"*What is the you who are living in the world?*"

> Answer:"*You are not living in this world. Nor is your ego (which is in this world) a separate thing that acts on its own, for that would mean you were split in two, with part of you on earth (ego) and part still in Heaven (spirit). Rather, you remain in Heaven,*[35] *in the constant state of immortality merely <u>believing</u> that you exist as an ego in this world.*"

Lisa B. Schermerhorn points out in her book *In Every Belief is a Lie,*[36] that the word *lie* is the center of the word *belief*. Our beliefs can lead us astray if we don't examine them carefully for the lies that are concealed within them. Our entire world's systems and structures are based upon the lie of separation.

---

[34] *A Course in Miracles, Circle of Atonement edition,* (2017), The Circle of Atonement, Inc., T-Ch 4, VIII, pg 181 footnote 85.
[35] I read this to mean that heaven is our identity Consciousness, which is why we *can* bring heaven to Earth.
[36] Lisa B. Schermerhorn, 2022, *In Every Belief is a Lie,* Lisa B. Schermerhorn.

> *"All that we see today that troubles is the expression of the story that I call separation."* —Charles Eisenstein[37]

We Are Not Small And Powerless

The CIA, Military and other arms of the Government have for years researched, trained and used people skilled in remote viewing,[38] who cultivate the power we all have as non-local Consciousness, to get information from within themselves connecting with anything anywhere. They can access information even in encoded form, from far away, through shielding, underwater, even in space, while being here on Earth. This information challenges and destroys our perception that we are separate from the world around us and localized to the body alone.

> *"There is no middleman between you and Source."*[39]
> —Alex Collier

A Course in Miracles says we exist *"in heaven, in a constant state of immortality."* What if we see ourselves as able to influence the happenings of this world? If we shift our worldview to the world being INSIDE of us, we can transform the world in leaps and bounds. A quantum shift of evolutionary advancement is possible when we release the straightjacket of limitation, which is what the belief that we are our bodies is. We are unlimited, capable and downright amazing! David Icke says we live in a physical simulation, and everything is created by the controllers of the simulation. Our factions, religions and skin color differences are all created. He says, "We really are all in this together as Divine Sparks of Infinite Awareness trapped in layers and layers of illusion."[40] This aligns

---

[37] Charles Eisenstein during interview with Andre Duqum, on 'Know Thyself' podcast, 8/22/2023 https://www.youtube.com/watch?v=h4zGuuCE5Yk
[38] Marc Newkirk's fourth talk 'Scientific Evidence of Metaphysical Truth' available on his son Ross's website www.ConsciousTechnologiesLLC.com.
[39] Interview of Alex Collier, with Dr. Christiane Northrup and Dr. Lee Merritt, https://www.alexcollier.org/dr-lee-merritt-and-dr-christiane-northrup-interview-alex-collier-november-2023/
[40] David Icke, 2023, *The Dream*, U.K.. Ickonic Publishing, pg 110.

with living *as*, *from* and *within* non-dual Consciousness. We can see the world's myriad of things as Consciousness (or Divine Spark) appearing as a thing. We can also focus upon the one still unchanging constant within all things and actions. Our clear sight focused upon the Consciousness within all things as we move through our day can transform our relationships and how we perceive the world. The outer world's changes do not need to affect us. We are whole and healed as Consciousness regardless of what is happening. Which assists us to see ourselves as valuable and equal to all others and part of the fabric of creation.

When I am in pain, I can expand my perspective to that of being Consciousness (instead of being my painful body) and ease the pain I feel by seeing the body as within me. The pain becomes an item of interest within me, not an all-consuming force. Try it the next time you are in pain. (The crucifixion and resurrection of Jesus was an extraordinary demonstration of this Truth of how one's Consciousness can outweigh and override the body's experience.)[41] By saying, "I am whole and complete," and by taking the time in quiet

> Say "I am whole and complete" at the first sign of sickness, injury or imbalance in the body, mind or spirit. Embody wholeness by seeing your body as within you.

to embody its meaning, my physical body often responds and throws off the whole idea of sickness. In practical terms, when I can hold that focus steadily enough, pain is lessened or completely dissolved. Ailments of the body, mind, emotions and spirit come from separation (our toxic misconception of ourselves as separate from everything that exists around us) and thus our ailments can be ameliorated or even averted at their source—which is Consciousness. Practicing this mind exercise and imagining our minds as able to heal, while seeing the illusory aspect of sickness, helps to create the strength of mind for this level of mastery

---

[41] See 'Jesus' commentary on the resurrection,' a received communication in the Appendix.

over our bodies. Mind strength is an important skill to cultivate, as it helps us stay focused upon our goals. Paramahansa Yogananda,[42] a Yogi able to heal with his hands and mind, said:

> *"The body is nothing but mind in action. There is no difference between the body and the mind except in their manifestations. . . . The physical affects the mental, and the mental affects the physical because they are interrelated. Therefore, you can affect the body through the mind or the mind through the body. Mind can enable you to do anything you want, but you must experiment first in little things until you fully develop that power."*

The whole world and our bodies are within Consciousness, as is the Mind. We influence everything, and everything influences us. Our identity is at the foundation of our life and environment. Imagine what our experience of living would be if we knew our world to be benevolent, joyous, loving and Whole. We would then assist in the creation of that kind of world.

> *"There can be no separation between the people of the Earth. They are of one mind and heart. The fabric of spiritual Consciousness runs through them all."*
> —Tom Brown, Jr. [43]

Oneness Holds Us to a Higher Standard

This knowledge of who we Truly are has its challenges, too, because it demands a higher level response from us. On a global level, our membership in the team of all life gifts us the opportunity to forgive, allow and not condemn. Correct error, yes, but condemn, no. It asks

---

[42] *Paramahansa Yogananda, (2005), Harmonizing Physical, Mental & Spiritual Methods of Healing,* How to Live Series No 1707, Self Realization Fellowship, pgs21-23.

[43] Tom Brown, Jr. (2007), *Grandfather,* Tracker Publishing, Audio Book Track 16,

us to operate from another set of Laws: Laws that are built upon peace, connection and that acknowledge our Oneness, and our role in the creation through our thoughts, emotions and actions. Self responsibility is a key foundation stone at this level. If we can see through what appears in the world and use a higher Law of Love to see with Love's sight, we create an opening for a higher outcome. It means taking ourselves less seriously, and remembering to laugh. It takes practice, willingness and is easier as more of us can manage to make this shift into our sight as Consciousness and Love.

On a personal level, when we feel hurt, betrayed or rejected, seeing the world through Love's perception as Consciousness gives us the opportunity to respond from our True Oneness and not from the body's subject/object pattern of projection,[44] judgment, accusation, blame and attack. This very personal opportunity to transform my perspective was given to me just yesterday by a friend, where I felt hurt and betrayed. I struggled to choose the highest road I could muster in forgiveness and wishing my friend well. It wasn't easy. I wanted to make him wrong, and the grace in the moment was that I could see that angry part of myself, feel the hurt *and* make the higher choice even with part of me kicking and screaming. It's a struggle, a process and a gateway. The more often we each can choose the higher road of who we really are, the easier it gets for all of us. Finding the path between this lofty perspective and our authenticity is the frontier of this time of transformation on Earth.

We must let go of everything that holds us to this world (the old Earth) to form the bridge of Love to the next one (the New Earth). It comes with letting go. So many attachments to the old world are born of fear, of littleness and of the idea of separation from God or Source. They do not serve on this New Earth. We are the sons and daughters of Eternal Life and we can reclaim our joy, happiness and the ultimate security of knowing who and what we are: Love incarnate in a Field of Love. That is what lies ahead when we can see.

---

[44] Our instinct is to *project* our own short falls upon others.

There is a winnowing process that will occur this coming year. If we embrace its every seeming loss with the armor of Love, and don't resist it, it will allow the breaking open of our hearts, so that all may feel and know their identity as Love incarnate, too. Our hearts broken open into a freer state, break others' hearts open to the light within us all. We *are* all *gifted with this opportunity. We can embrace it fully.* Like the Native American Hopi Prophecy[45] says, *"We are the ones we have been waiting for."*

Breaking open to a new level of vulnerability, forgiveness, willingness and Love is presenting itself now. As wars are breaking out and our Earth is in danger, more and more people are seeing the futility of this way of being. Peace begins within us. It's a choice we can learn to make. This section of the **EARTHwise Constitution** helps to clarify what it means to live from and as Consciousness:

> 6.1 Act from Unitive Consciousness. Life is a unified reality, and so are living systems. To architect, design, and steward for thrivability means to act from unitive consciousness, with care for each other and the Earth.
>
> 6.1.0 Start from the premise that consciousness is primary and foundational. Consciousness is who we all are, and not something we have or own.
>
> 6.1.1 Dispel the illusion of separation. Life is informationally unified at all levels and scales of existence.
>
> 6.1.2 Honor our unity in diversity and the interdependence of being.[46]

---

[45] The Hopi Prophecy in a fuller form is in the Appendix. https://artistic.umn.edu/we-are-ones-weve-been-waiting-prophecy-made-hopi-elders

[46] https://www.earthwisecentre.org/constitution, pg 23. Please look up this beautiful and thoughtful Constitution and consider sharing it widely.

In Joseph Chilton Pearce's book *The Biology of Transcendence,* he describes a state of "unconflicted behavior," where his perspective was from beyond the fear of death (a complete letting go, as described above). It allowed Pearce to do things normally impossible, like intentionally and repeatedly burn himself with a cigarette with no pain or repercussions—his skin was unharmed. It would seem from his stories that all of our conflicts of behavior that keep us outside of miraculous capabilities are conflicts that separate us from our divine essence, source or power. Our misidentification as being just a body intensifies the disconnect more, and places obstacles to these kinds of capacities in our way. Taken to the extreme, this perspective of unconflicted behavior, offers unlimited physical capabilities, where nothing can harm or hurt us. Vedanta explains that we have three bodies: gross, subtle and causal.[47] Our physical body is visible, the other two are not. The subtle body includes our sense organs and how they interact with the world. It is experiencable to ourselves, but not to others. The causal body is what the gross and subtle bodies revert into when we drop the physical body. I wonder if Pearce's state of unconflicted behavior is our purest, truest original self, the causal body in charge of the physical and subtle bodies, demonstrating that we can transcend limitations of the body and mind and embody a higher opportunity for mankind. These higher frequency times asks of us to reach and stretch for these kinds of expanded human potentials to break us away from limitations of all kinds. I find it helpful to have a conceptual framework to explain phenomenal behavior such as this, that could explain walking on water, raising from death, amazing strength and invulnerability in battle, all demonstrations of how our Oneness outside of the grasp of fear and death, gives us a higher physical possibility.

Every last thing is connected and interpenetrating, and hence we influence it all and it influences us. Our opportunity is to transcend all separating projections, overlays and images, and to acknowledge that

---

[47] *Swami Paramarthananda of Chennai, (2019), Vedanta the Big Picture,* Monce IL, pg.41.

glorious divine essence in all Life, that Consciousness is who we are, and we need not be subject to all the Earthly Laws all the time.

Transhumanism

With the splicing of a human body with technology,[48] a digital force enters our bodies. The digital force has no heart, and it may bring a loss of feeling and compassion for others, to the human who is hosting the digital force. With this possibility, it appears like the rules of "what a human is" have changed. But perhaps, this need not be the case. There is a healing that may occur as the Oneness of all Life is acknowledged and aligned with … as we see a transhuman as one of the very many fractals of One Source. The human part of a transhuman is from the same source that we are. It is this unifying factor that will help us to see with Love any situation before us. Not all beings will find and be able to hold onto, their unified spark of God/Creator's Light, with the influence of the digital presence, but many, many will. It is this chance that we must hold onto, and hold out for, for it is in the union of Life on Earth that much more will become possible that never was here before. We can be still in knowing that there is a unity inherent within all beings, human and transhuman. Expecting it to become conscious in all is not likely at this current frequency on Earth. As time goes on however, our unity will become increasingly evident and will be the secret sauce that makes another level of interaction and Love more possible. Hold onto this vision, even through times of difficulty. Hold onto the Love that we are in alignment with—the Light of Consciousness that shines through all beings. It is not to say to align with a transhuman's form or beliefs; it is to hold steady, focus upon that which is good and great and true, and see it everywhere and in all beings— human and transhuman. With this gaze of Light, miracles can occur.

---

[48] At Whole Foods store in Denver yesterday there was a "pay with your palm" option. They will connect your palm's image with your name, credit card and other data. Modern conveniences may, down the road, use this kind of technology to limit and control us further.

I take a moment to imagine a transhuman in front of me. It gives me a foothold into compassion with the focus upon what we both share—our humanity, and the eternality within our humanity, that joins us together. I venture to say that in having this capacity and willingness to stand in Love (not *projecting our Love onto* someone else), simply within ourselves, *knowing Love is all around us* and within us, and within them (even if it is not evident), we can call legions of help to our side if needed.

We bring coherence to our energy field with love and peaceful acceptance. The Heartmath Institute[49] has done much research on this phenomenon. They have developed techniques that help the heart come into coherence and regulate the brain, and observed how a more coherent heart field influences the less coherent hearts around us. Love is a steadying influence, Love looks for reasons to Love. Fear looks for guilt and to blame others. Our opportunity is to be authentic,[50] to communicate what we need, hold ourselves and others accountable for their actions, and create a world that reflects the Truth of who we are as interconnected sparks of eternal Life, Light and Love.

---

[49] HeartMath Institute https://www.heartmath.org/
[50] Merriam Webster's most popular word in 2023 was "authentic,' this is a good sign of humanity's consciousness rising.

I created this image after I was alone in my house with my small children, and I heard some noises that made me afraid. I call it *"When I Asked For Protection They Showed Me This."*

It's an image of magnificent guardian Angels of Light surrounding a house. It's illustrative of an unseen reality and potential that is with us and free for the asking. Angels such as these are our brethren in Consciousness. Prayer, chanting, envisioning and calls for help can be a medium of communication with the Consciousness that enlivens other beings and our Source, possibly giving us the perspective to bypass a potentially adversarial encounter. How we see and perceive the situation can bring others to a more open-hearted perspective. By opening our hearts other hearts can open.

The transhuman situation, where the will and actions of some humans may be taken over, may require us to retreat into hiding for a period until the frequency rises further on Earth. In the face of this possibility we need to hold our frequency high and stay grounded and in connection with our Source. In staying grounded and fully inhabiting our bodies, we will know what to do in any moment. Our bodies are embedded within the natural world and can help guide our actions too.

I don't know how all this will play out. Do you? Take a moment and look at the paths you see for life on Earth. What do they look like? What qualities do they exhibit? Which path do you wish to walk forward onto? Pour your energy into that path. Love is a bridge to a higher-world possibility for humanity. The quality of Love I am referring to here is strong, clear, coherent, resourceful and potent, and transcends limits of all kinds!

Consciousness or "the spirit that moves through all things" is the thread that connects us all, enlivens us, loves us, and powers our Love. Loving this Consciousness is a boon to our lives. It's a doorway that can change how we see this world's people and material objects. How we view things can make a huge difference in what happens.

> *"The beliefs you hold are your jailers or your wings to freedom. ....You live as the Being you imagine you are. Imagination is the powerhouse of your inner God when aligned to Truth, Oneness and Source."*-- The Key To Love: A Teaching From The Beings Of Light[51]

With this knowledge, people smile at you. Miracles are logical, ordinary and abundant.

---

[51] Hope Ives Mauran, (2016), *The Key To Love: A Teaching From The Beings Of Light*, NY, The Legwork Team.

CH III NATURE'S LAWS OF CREATION

*Unless something depends on undivided guidance,
it cannot approach human beings as an experience of nature
through sensory perceptions. —Rudolph Steiner* [52]

Our divine spark of creativity often lies latent, languishing unused as we deal with the daily routines of life—eat, work, sleep and repeat. Now we can value and feed our creativity as we are entrusted with the great work of creating a New Earth Paradigm. When we join together with a shared focus and pure intent, miracles become commonplace. We have the wind of the Universe at our backs when we create *from*, *with* and *for* Love. In some beautiful way we lift out of the old world (of separation, victimhood and competition) and into the New, a world of Oneness, self-responsibility and cooperation. Our tools for creation begin with our identity as Consciousness appearing as a human, the knowledge of the natural Laws, and our deep and heartfelt desire for a more loving New Earth reality.

Creating From Wholeness vs Separation in Order to Know

The statistics, case studies, data and information we so revere often determines what we believe about ourselves and the world. The sciences generally use the process of *separation-in-order-to-know*. They isolate one

---

[52] Rudolph Steiner, (2003), The Reappearance of Christ in The Etheric, a collection of lectures on The Second Coming of Christ: USA, Steiner Books, pgs.178-179.

variable to study it, hoping to find its static ultimate reality. Anastasia, the remarkable woman who lives in the remote Taiga of Siberia, whose purity and capacities are beyond our modern day comprehension,[53] said that humanity's fall out of the Garden of Eden of Wholeness into separation came when we started trying to understand how the Creator of this world made such a perfect Creation. We went astray when we started tearing its wholeness apart in an attempt to understand its perfection, synergy and power in order to claim it for ourselves. She said it is similar to having a beautiful working car, and deciding to start taking it apart to find out how it works, instead of hopping in and enjoying its ride. Science tends to ignore the integrity and power of the wholeness of the world, and that the world needs the integrity of all its parts to maintain its wholeness.

> *A mind that is limited to reason and analysis is incapable of perceiving what is truth."*
>
> —J. Krishnamurti

Traditional science ignores the reality of the world's intrinsic *whole-already* perfection. Robin Wall Kimerer, a Native American Scientist, in *The Sun* magazine explained an expanded approach quite elegantly: "The idea is to pay attention to the living world as if it were a spider's web; when you touch one part, the whole web responds. Experimental, hypothesis-driven science looks just at that one point you touched." The Earth is not a machine. We cannot assume that a formula for our creations will produce what we want like a factory. Instead of deferring our creative power to the scientific experts, to governments, to (self-proclaimed) global leaders and their statistics, we can acknowledge that we have an innate wholeness as Consciousness that already knows how to manage, live in and participate in the world. Be kind, respect nature, love one another, create in alignment with the dictate of "do no harm," be grateful, have a relationship of reciprocity with the Earth and all life, be still, and observe before acting etc.. When we *experience* something to gain knowledge, we own that knowledge far more solidly

---

[53] Vladimir Megre's, (1996), *Co-Creation. The Ringing Cedars Series, Hawaii, Ringing Cedars Press. Book 4.*

than if we learn it from a book or lecture. No high school, college or graduate degrees are necessary to have the skills, gifts, talents and moral code for creation with the natural world. From open and loving hearts, with our focus upon what we *do want,* nothing need stop us from living in harmony with each other and the Earth. Sometimes the experts tell us all the reasons why we can't … why something can't be done, transformed, created or cleaned up. However, with our knowledge of the Field of Love, our identity as Consciousness, the mastery of these Laws of Creation, and respect for Nature, far more is possible than linear, five-senses-bound science allows for.

The observer influences the experiment[54] This world is one grand experiment that we can influence. It is our opportunity to see cooperation, beauty, love, harmony and unity, and transform what we see by how we see it. It reminds me of the rice experiment.

Put cooked rice in three jars. One is a control, one you send love to, and one you hate.[55] When my friend Lisa did this with her young boys, the one they hated turned black very soon. The control held out for quite a bit longer. The one they loved lasted for many, many *years*! It appears as though *Love puts matter outside of the aging process, lifting it to a higher order of the Laws of Nature.* If Loving from the outside of something can transform it in this way, imagine what *embodiment* of Love can do from our expanded perspective as Consciousness itself. It makes me excited to think of the possibilities for us all in this regard. Allow your self to feel this Love throughout your body.

There is also a phenomenon where a very holy, loving person's body doesn't decay after death. The *incorruptible body*[56] is a phenomenon

---

[54] As I understand the double slit experiment, light can be either a particle or a wave, and acts differently in different observer situations. https://en.wikipedia.org/wiki/Double-slit_experiment,

[55] https://www.masteryintheartofliving.com/creating-positive-work-and-home-environments-with-intention/

[56] Joan Carroll Cruz, (1977) "The Incorruptibles," Tan Books, offers an overview of the topic.

wherein dead bodies many hundreds of years old are as fresh and supple as they were upon burial. This can occur regardless of the use of quick lime to speed decay of the body, moisture and the use of other catalysts for decomposition. Some of the bodies that were exhumed were discovered to be fresh, even smell of a beautiful perfume and some even bleed. This phenomenon has no official explanation. It appears to me that the pure Love of the Divine Source Creator that these holy people exhibited, and their unbroken connection to Source their spark of infinity (or eternality) give their cells eternal life. Love is the ultimate power, and it is what prevails upon this Earth. Its presence is ours to acknowledge and embrace and embody.

A Cause and Effect Reality

It's easy to forget our role in what happens around us because the causes and effects in this 3D world are separated by time. Our every act influences our environment and is added to the collective of human creations. We are not powerless or ineffectual. Each one of us can make a positive difference. When we join together, our power is multiplied. Treading lightly upon the Earth is also recommended for that same reason as well, because our negative combined impact adds up, too—like the plastic waste piling up in dumps, landfills and the oceans.

Nature's Laws are supportive, consistent, predictable, immutable and undivided. They, like eternal undivided Consciousness, are behind our lives and fully support us whether we believe in them or not. Nature's Laws are a complex energetic, quantum, heart-full algorithm. They apply even to those of us who live in the city, in an apartment without a tree in sight. We are all embedded within Nature's perfect system that creates and has created everything we see around us. This chapter outlines the four basic Laws of Creation: Attraction, Deliberate Intent, Allowing and Harmony. Positive creation is catalyzed by our spontaneous, high frequency, inspired, passionate imagining, envisioning and dreaming. Spontaneity is a potent aspect of initiating the creative process; it is pure in origin.

Our *desire* moves into *energy*, then physical *manifestation*. Understanding what the Laws are and cultivating our use of them is a stepping stone *into* active participation with creation. Imagine playing chess without knowing the rules, or acting in a play without knowing your lines. You would be a poor player or performer. We are already an integral part of the world around us. When we know the Laws, we can be more helpful in actively choosing to create a better planetary experience for all. The knowledge of how to create needs to be taught in schools. Humanity used to have this knowledge, but it has been lost, hidden, buried or destroyed in recent centuries. Perhaps the killing of witches and other *keepers of the knowledge of who we are* and the *knowledge of how creation works* was purposely and blatantly done in previous centuries, and done more subtly now,[57] to remove this creative power and opportunity from humanity's knowledge base and direct experience.

This quote from *Handbook for the New Paradigm, Book III Becoming*[58] speaks about the use of these Laws:

> *The key to the application is in knowing that the intent must be in harmony with the flow of expansive creative energies that move and carry the manifestation of galaxies, solar systems, planets and individuals through to experience creation in the observation mode. It is necessary to understand that* **all that is considered reality first begins in the imagination, the mind of the conceiver.** [emphasis added] *The focus of intent moves the process through the various stages of conception to energy conversion resulting in coagulation of that energy by slowing down the vibration until it manifests into observable, touchable matter or what is called manifested reality. What is considered reality is focused intent condensed through*

---

[57] Modern day scientist, inventors, and thinkers that create next-level advanced technologies, have had their inventions destroyed, their labs ransacked, and their invention confiscated. Unfortunately Nicola Tesla, Victor Schauberger, Wilhelm Reich and many others fall into this category.

[58] *Becoming*, Volume III, Hayden ID, Bridger House Publishers, INC., pg.106.

> *application of the Universal laws by holding the intent firmly and "knowing" that the process works (until it does). The slower the vibration of the focusing mind and the surrounding environment, the longer the process takes and the more difficult it is to hold the intent long enough. Learning through application to hold the intent "lightly" without attempting to force its creation but again in "knowing" the validity of the process allows for "practice makes perfect."*

Machele Small Wright[59] wrote about manifesting a garden shovel into physical form in this manner.[60] It was misshapen at first try and disappeared after awhile. It requires practice to create in this way, with clear intent, mental intensity and focus.

Here are the four Natural Laws that I have freely lifted and elaborated upon, from the *Handbook for the New Paradigm* series.[61] These Laws are a key to our release from whatever limitations we find ourselves in. Think of something that you have successfully created in your life—a project, a new business, a repair of something, or a meal. Think through the process you went through, your own process of creation as you read these laws, and see where the Laws help you to understand the creation process at a practical level. You have used these laws already, unconsciously and on purpose, they are natural to us. This is an opportunity now to understand them more fully *in service to the New Earth, our shared community of Life and the human family.* Some might consider these laws a self-help technique. They are far beyond that. They are intrinsic to the creative process of life, and are at the very core of what it means to be human. Learning them helps our co-creation of a positive future

---

[59] Link to 'Perelandra Center for Nature Research.' https://perelandra-ltd.com/
[60] Machele Small Wright, author of *Behaving as if the God in All Life Mattered*, I believe this book is the one in which she wrote of these experiences. In her book *Dancing on the Far Side of the Moon*, she chronicles living a life on another planet, while her body on Earth is sleeping.
[61] *Embracing the Rainbow*, 2nd book in the *Handbook for the New Paradigm* Series, Idaho, Bridger House Publishing.

together, and it's the way we will manifest Love's New Earth beneath our feet. *Not in a potential future, but right here and now.*

Nature's 1st Law is Attraction or Frequency. Like attracts like, and opposites attract (they are two sides of the same coin). Animals of one species hang out together. People do the same with like-minded people, talkative people attract quiet listeners. I even find that my Phillips head screwdrivers accumulate together! It's a natural organizing flow of life. In the way that patterns are created when sound is applied to a surface covered in sand (as demonstrated by Cymatics),[62] a complex, frequency-based organizing system creates form, occurrences and interrelationships. This is one level of creation that is occurring beneath the surface of life. We attract what is like our frequency from the level of our emotions, thoughts, minds, beliefs, ideas, past actions, experiences, woundings, and who knows what else! An organizing hand, formula, algorithm, frequency, vibration, dream or idea orchestrates all that happens, and the patterns, events and results that occur. They are orderly, synchronistic and quite brilliant. Its results are individual, collective, consistent and creative, and also the results are changeable by us when we shift our frequency and focus. This world also has octaves of density where worlds exist simultaneously within the same spaces. Miracles, tragedies and the mundane are all demonstrations of this Law. Our Love and joy attract more of the same quality experiences in life; and fear, guilt, shame and similar things attract their like. Gratitude attracts things to be grateful for. Loving attracts love. Many of the spiritual practices (such as breathing, meditation, puja, yoga, Tai Chi, and Chi Gung) are practices that over time raise our vibration and thus what we attract, experience and project into Life.

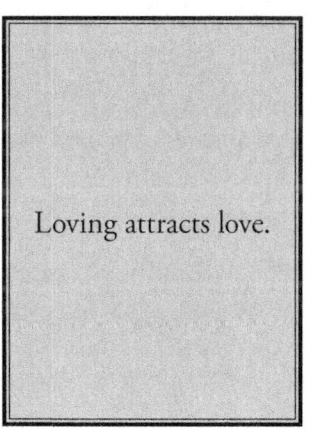
Loving attracts love.

---

[62] Hans Jenny, 2001, *Cymatics*, Newmarket NH, MACROmedia publishing.

"Frequencies are feelings. If you are trying to shift your frequency you just need to shift your feelings." — Penny Kelly, *Look-See*, November 2023

"The simplest way to begin practicing higher consciousness is to understand that beauty, honesty, compassion, a sense of humor, creativity, generosity, are all higher vibration approaches to life. Anger, vengeance, selfishness, fear, resentment, meanness, destructiveness, are all in a much lower vibration. The first step into higher consciousness is to stop contributing to lower consciousness. — Penny Kelly, *Look-See*, November 2023

Nature's 2nd Law is Deliberate Intent, wherein we actively choose our focus without wavering or falling into old, idle or negative thought patterns. The images we create in great detail in our minds attract their materiality. When the ideas we have come with a spark of joy that lights our fire of endeavor, we ignite a process of creation in communication with the Field of Love and Life all around us. *Creative intentions are spontaneous, fast and natural.* They are created from our innermost longings and the natural expression of the fullness of who we are, not always from slower linear thought. Speaking our intent transcends space and time, and cause and effect.[63] Our mind is a powerful virtual-reality headset, allowing us to visualize and create. When we create, we become blind to the things we don't want, and disengage from the old patterns, as we reinforce, choose and see only what we *do* want. We then create a new pattern, a new blueprint, a new image within the "Cosmic lattice". *We don't have to know how we will achieve what we imagine*: this second Law takes our vision and runs with it. Our task is to have our *intent* and *focus* upon what we *do* want, to pull our creation forth from a potential future, in detail and precision. "Where

---

[63] *Speaking into Existence: The Power of Vowels and the Science of Attraction*, based on the book
The Power of Vowels, by Michael Tellinger https://www.youtube.com/watch?v=Ij8T1QCPY7I

our attention goes, energy flows."[64] Allow the Field of Infinite Potential to assist your ideas into form. The Field of Infinite Potential exists. You might call it Nature's Warehouse—or the limitless Void. All possibilities exist within it. The building blocks for anything and everything are there in potential. Our desire, passion and intent draw from that deep, dark reservoir and mysteriously bring experiences and things into our physical world.

> *"Pure intent draws from the Cosmic lattice to create life change."*[65]
> — Kryon, a spiritual non-physical entity channeled by Lee Caroll

In the synchronicity of my meeting Sarah in Chapter I, my unspoken desire to meet her had a lightness to it. It wasn't a heavy need, just a casual, authentic wondering about her that these laws made happen when her package was delivered to my porch. The Universal Laws conspire for the highest outcome. You can trust them. They have integrity. For that reason, when we launch a verbal, emotional or mental intention, yearning, desire or thought, adding in "*. . . if it be for the highest and best good of all concerned*"[66] is an excellent qualifier that helps us ensure the best possible result, because we can't possibly know all the variables in play. It allows creation itself to show its resourcefulness, creativity and glory beyond what we can imagine or create for ourselves while avoiding the pitfalls pointed to in the maxim "Be careful what you wish for; you just might get it!"

> *"The value of deciding in advance what you want to happen is simply that you will perceive the situation as a means to make it happen. You will therefore make every effort to overlook what interferes with the accomplishment*

---

[64] Nicole Matoushek, MPH, PT, 2009, *What I Forgot The Day I Was Born*, USA, Xlibris Corporation.

[65] Lee Carroll, *Kryon Book VII, Energy Creation*, excerpts originally taken from pages 238-243.

[66] *Handbook for the New Paradigm*, Bridger House Publishers Inc. Idaho.

of your objective, and concentrate on everything that helps you to meet it." —A Course In Miracles, ACOA, Ch 17, VI,4,1-2

Nature's 3rd Law is Allowing. After a deliberate intent has been launched, birthed, planted, seeded or ignited in the Cosmic lattice and handed off to Nature's Warehouse foreman, the next step is to *allow*. Allow the Universe or Nature to do its part. Step back. Like an archer chooses an arrow, aims and releases it to its target, the creation process is similar. We allow the arrow to fly: once we release it, our work is done; we cannot influence it further until it hits the target. If the target is missed, we can then try another arrow of desire (another image, idea or goal). Allowing requires the wisdom of knowing when to act and when not to act. When a souffle is in the oven cooking, opening the oven to check on it causes it to collapse. In Allowing, you let your creations form and grow. Like planting seeds, Nature takes over after you have deliberately created the conditions that will ensure their growth, and you let time do its job until they germinate and peek above the ground. Nature is in charge of that part. The stillness of Allowing must eventually move back into action when you re-engage with the active part of the creative process.

> After you have put in your order at the Universal Diner, don't be an impatient customer and ask "Is it ready yet?"

It's really not up to us. That is what this law is saying. We are part of a team that includes all and everything. Allowing the results and just getting on with life is sometimes the perfect Allowing that the Universe needs, and it may not be what you had in mind. Nature doesn't need or want your help at this stage of the process, so get out of the kitchen, let it go, while remaining attuned for your internal (kitchen) timer that tells you when you need to do something further . . . And that is where the Fourth Law, Harmony, comes in.

The 4th Law is Harmony (or Flow). Harmony results after the first 3 steps are engaged—Attraction, Intention, Allowing and then Harmony. Harmony is a fluid synergy of alignment. We feel it when it is present. It is a desired state that brings ease to our physical world and is the final stage of the creative process. It is natural and our task is to recognize it, be grateful for it and *support it*. Our Harmony meter is internal. We know it when we feel and see it as we move through our day. We can feel internally when we are doing the *right* next thing, *and* when we are doing the *wrong* next thing. Paying attention to the subtle inner promptings of our lives and acting on them brings Harmony. When we are outside of the harmonious flow of life, we are swimming upstream. You know that feeling you get when you need to apologize or when you make a mistake or when you ought to make a business call that you are avoiding? It's that kind of niggling disturbance that prompts your apology, corrective action or call, and a return to harmony. Harmony doesn't mean everything is easy or comfortable. Nature is the great steward of Harmony. You can see it in a mature forest of stately trees, streams, mossy rocks and animals: there is order, peace, coexistence and Harmony. It is not all a hodgepodge. Even though there are millions of life forms present, they are working together and Harmony is present. We are also aware of a lack of Harmony and can make choices to avoid a situation based upon Harmony's absence, or work to help Harmony to be present.

Marc Newkirk illustrated the four Laws well in a talk he gave[67] where he shared a video of a man participating in a spoon bending event organized by Jack Houck,[68] with twenty-five people learning to bend spoons. The frequency was high in the room because there were *many people with the same intention*, creating a coherency in the energy in the room (Law #1). The man focused on the spoon with the intention that it would break apart as he pulled it in opposite directions (Law

---

[67] https://www.conscioustechnologiesllc.com/resources, Marc Newkirk's lecture is called Scientific Evidence of Metaphysical Truth. All his talks are worth watching. This website is Ross Newkirk's, (Marc's son).

[68] Jack is the originator of Psychokinesis (PK) Parties, and is recognized as one of the foremost authorities in the world on the subject. https://www.jackhouck.com/

#2). When he *abruptly stopped focusing upon it,* it released into allowing (Law #3). That's when the spoon pulled apart easily.[69] The separated spoon pieces were the harmonious result (Law #4). We also can potentize the Field of Love (that all this world exists within) in the same way when we join together in creating a shared goal—in this case creating a New Earth paradigm. You could say it's a miracle to bend or break a spoon like butter. If twenty-five people coming together can do this, imagine what we all can do to transform our world. Have you ever experienced a field effect that was coherent and high frequency in a similar way?

What I realize in the Laws of Nature is that there is great Love in them. They are moral and just and create stability, like the four legs on a table. The First Law, A*ttraction,* brings us what we *already are.* The Second Law, *Deliberate Intent,* allows us to call forth *our heart's desire* with intention, to change course, or build and expand upon what we have attracted. With the Third Law, *Allowing,* Nature, the Universe or the Creator God meets us halfway—*we don't have to do it all ourselves;* we are acknowledging we are part of a team. The Fourth Law, *Harmony,* is the result as equilibrium returns and where our partnership and responsibility for our creations kick in. We need to evaluate what we have created: Is it suitable and non-harming? What could be more simple, supportive and loving than these four Laws? Uniquely suited for creation ourselves, we are not victims of the world; we are an integral part of the natural world on Earth. We all have the power to engage and create *as part of the team* of life. The Universe is guiding our actions, knows us intimately, and when we act with the four Laws, and Cause and Effect in mind,[70] our ability to create is empowered. The Laws have been here all along. They have been used to create the positive and negative systems of life that we are living within now.

---

[69] A spoon just like it was tested, and it required 800 pounds of force to break it apart.

[70] Mark Passio's Documentary, *The Science of Natural Law.* https://onegreatworknetwork.com/mark-passio/mark-passio-the-science-of-natural-law

We are answerable for our creations. Our actions are impacting all that surrounds us, each other and the Earth, in this moment and for all time. It's helpful to note that our emotional ups and downs don't thwart or endanger our ability to create. What is created and its quality and how, when and where it's created, is ultimately decided by Nature. We do have the opportunity (and obligation) to influence the creation for the better. I do think it is why we are all here. At this momentous time of mass awakening, we can help change the direction the societies are moving in, by respecting Nature and seeding higher frequency images, into the Cosmic lattice.

Our creativity, spontaneity and nurturing can fill in its details. What we can *imagine,* is possible to create upon a New Earth. Curiously, our work now is also to disengage from the old world. If we stop feeding it, it will disappear sooner. We can't pursue two opposite futures at the same time. We need to choose which one we will talk about, focus on, engage with, create and experience.

In choosing to create a New Earth Paradigm, "all is well" is an anchoring energy and thought that supports the process. It might be tempting to get caught up in the chaos and destruction energy of the old world paradigm falling away. It's best to cultivate the peace of "all is well."[71] I feel greater ease in my body just thinking about it. Do You? It's a solid foundation for the New Earth to be built upon. As Consciousness all *is* well!

All life is an orderly and also an ecstatic dance of communion upon this Earth. There are the main laws and there are more subtle aspects to them. It is actually not imperative to know these Laws. It is important, however, to align with the Wholeness that underlies the Laws and their exactitude. They are exact in that there is no wiggle room to exceptionalize the parts of them that are inconvenient for us on a certain day.

---

[71] *Handbook for the New Paradigm, Becoming, Book III,* Idaho. Bridger House Publisher, Inc.

The Laws accrue: what we do and don't do accumulates effects, day after day like karma.[72] Although there are ways to transcend the Laws, they are not actually ever set aside; *even the miraculous is Lawful.* So knowing this, enjoy this Life, study the Laws and see what results as our frequency rises and life is more and more joyful.

> Turn off the TV, radio, news and movies because external images are being planted in your mind's eye, commandeering your creative power.

The playbook for the game of life is all around us. We can open our eyes, soften our perspective and recognize that what is happening in the world, as Consciousness *"is an ecstatic dance of communion upon Earth."* Our Oneness is dancing together with itself in all our different forms. We can see cause and effect in action. We can see how one's *way of seeing* the world colors what occurs. This potent moment in time is our cosmic opportunity to end human suffering, war, abuse, slavery and the destruction of the Earth, by consciously creating a New Earth based in Love, using these Laws, from the *inside* of Oneness Consciousness and with the rising frequency of the Earth.

In Truth, Love's New Earth exists *already* as the potential future for each of us. Breathe that in for a moment. As one of us chooses it, it becomes easier for the rest of us to find it. What we are actually doing is bringing it from the future into right now, collapsing time.[73] Or perhaps you could say we are uncovering it[74] from where it has been all along, hidden from our sight. The physics of reality include time and space. Space and what appears as matter within it are mostly just empty space when you look at the smaller and smaller "particles" that make up

---

[72] "Karma is not a punishment. Karma is an electromagnetic record of everything that has happened on the planet. Just as there are high and low notes in music, or colors ranging from infrared to ultraviolet, in the same way human vibrations can be divided into high and low frequencies. Everything in our world vibrates at one frequency or another." -author unknown.

[73] *Becoming*, Bridger House Publisher, Inc. Idaho.

[74] David Icke, *The Dream*, pg 323.

material form. So what appears as solid matter is mostly empty space popping in and out of existence. Time actually consists of only now. The past and the future are concepts that are helpful for us as physical beings, but they don't actually exist. So time and space are pretty fluid in a sense, because they are not encumbered by the constructs of past and future that we have used to orient ourselves in this world. This knowledge of how fluid it all is helps us to stay relaxed in the saddle and to respond to life in real time.

Jumping Timelines

The idea of *jumping timelines* came to my attention recently. It is a phenomenon whereby we shift the thread of our lives to a parallel or alternative one that exists already, based upon our frequency and focus. Perhaps we can encourage a spontaneous jump to higher and better futures if we can match our actions, emotions, thoughts, etc., to the ones that are in that higher frequency timeline. Have you ever had that feeling that there was something "new" about a familiar place? Penny Kelly shared a story[75] of a couple who were on the highway when a rock hit the windshield of their car and cracked it. When they used the car a few days later the crack was not there. She suggested that they had shifted timelines. In the comments below Penny's online video, a person shared that they were looking at the clock when it said 4:44. As they were watching it, it went to 4:43, and then again after a minute to 4:44. This person also shared going to take a nap in their bedroom with the door closed, while the cat slept on their chest. When they awoke, the cat was in another room with the door closed, with no way it could have gotten out of the bedroom and

> Keep all technology out of your bedroom and turn off your cell phone and the WIFI router at night.

---

[75] Penny Kelly's November 2023 Look See, available on YouTube.https://www.youtube.com/watch?v=VBlmqxTMdl4

into the other room. The concept of multiple parallel realities unfolding simultaneously cracks the solidity of this world apart.

Could it be that we can hop back and forth, in and out of different futures? Yes, this is definitely a possibility. The time lines of planet Earth have been engineered to include many, many potentials, as the world is unfolding and the land mass is transforming to higher levels of energy. It is more and more possible to harmonize with higher or lower parallel realities that might show us a different reality, friend group, way of life, even opportunities existing upon other planets. (That can be a distraction however.) For our purposes it is best to realize that there is choice and kismet[76] involved. If our intent is to inhabit the highest possible timeline for our life stream, we need to make the changes and choices necessary for this to manifest. All of creation bends and flows to our formulations of desire and our incarnated Wholeness.

If we choose Love's New Earth, that intention has got to speed its presence into our experience.

I entered *Love's New Earth* today as I drove over the rise on Rte12 South, entering Putnamville, Vermont. I had just read *The Transition Plan for a Thrivable Civilization*[77] by Anneloes Smitsman, PhD. It made me so excited when I realized that there are many intelligent and courageous people focused upon the New Earth's creation. In the present and eternal moment of now I realized that the New Earth is here already right now. Since then I have been on the lookout for signs of the New Earth, so that I can acknowledge and celebrate it. On a long journey from Florida to Maine, I saw two signs of the New Earth. One was outside a church in Florida—"Hey You, You are loved!"—and the other was on the drive home from the airport—"Spread Love Everywhere You Go." This is the time to call forth the highest vision for life on Earth,

---

[76] Kismet definition from online Merriam Webster Dictionary: a hypothetical force or personified power that determines the course of the future events.
[77] https://medium.com/earthwise-stories/transition-plan-for-a-thrivability-civilisation-116ff754d710, Transition Plan For A Thrivable Civilization, Anneloes Smitsman, PhD.

with Love as its foundation. Its creation starts inside of us and our expectation that the New Earth is here already right now, miraculously lands us solidly upon it.

This story illustrated how the rising frequency on Earth is conspiring to help the creation of Love's New Earth. A year ago, an acupuncturist, shared that she had adopted her now elderly dog off the streets of Boston. As I lay on her acupuncture table, it suddenly dawned on me that we really ought to also be adopting *people* off the streets, not just the dogs! That seed idea took root, and one morning six months later, I saw a homeless woman in town. I struck up a conversation with her and ended up inviting her to stay with me sometime, if she wanted to. We traded numbers and she came to stay on and off throughout the summer for two or three nights at a time. Her expectation was to get subsidized housing in the summer. It took many more months of her focused intent and action upon housing to actually get it. She was deliberate, persistent and had help. She allowed the process to unfold and harmony gave her a happy ending. She is an artist, working towards having her own show, and is now safe and off the streets, having moved into an apartment just this week. We are all magnificent creators no matter where we live.

In the same way that I imagine pioneer women in the American West created the modern day supermarkets by day dreaming about an easier life as they were working in a hard one, visionaries, mystics and *all of us* can seed the future. with our own dreams and visions of a Love-based Earth culture where homelessness is unheard of, and where energy is free. We are powerful. We can fill in the details, take loving actions beyond what we did on the old Earth in the past, and live upon the New Earth starting right now. No waiting. We can begin today as our emotions experience *having it already*. We feel it in our bodies and (as our emotion is of *having it already*) we are upon it. Our New Earth is incompatible with our lingering focus upon the negative attributes of old Earth. We will naturally pop back and forth between Earths for awhile. When I notice I have slipped back into a negative energy and viewpoint, I choose again to inhabit and see the New Earth. It's lighter, more joyful, peaceful and beautiful. We may still be *doing* the exact same things, tending to work, family and other life obligations but how we feel and the meaning we give to what we see completely changes. Continuing to focus upon the old Earth captures our energy and we remain within it.

There are no barriers to entry in creation for a human, it is our nature. No permission is necessary. When we look outside of ourselves to an external authority that we assume is greater in some way, we ignore our own knowledge of what this world could be, and we thwart our creative ability. It is our birthright to create a thriving and healthy planet. We have simply been asleep at the wheel for a long time here, and we are now being shaken awake by the world around us, to get back into the driver's seat of this bus of humanity that is careening out of control! We can actively steer towards a New Earth paradigm based in Love, where no one is homeless or hungry. And if someone is, we make it our business to help them. In this new reality we don't look outside of ourselves for the solutions; we work locally and sometimes unofficially to change whatever causes these situations of lack.

Images from Elsewhere

I have noticed that when an inspired thought comes to mind, it comes like a bullet train passing through the station. Our capacity to think with speed,[78] focus, power and clarity has dwindled. Perhaps the television was created to keep us sitting passively in the bleachers of life and not playing the game of creation.

Our current world is saturated with images that arise from *someone else's mind*. Distractions and information that overloads us abound. Beings who have faster and clearer speed of thought and who understand the Laws of Creation can out-create us.[79] They are in charge of the media. An endless news stream blocks, distorts and overpowers our own visions

---

[78] *Vladimir Megre, Co-Creation*, The Ringing Cedars of Russia Series.
[79] *Vladimir Megre, Co-Creation*, The Ringing Cedars of Russia Series.

and ideas. Why not take a break from phones, radios, TVs, news and social media, movies, Netflix, virtual reality headsets, computers, etc.? The images and frequencies of these devices can draw us outside of our own bodies and make space for foreign thoughts and entities to insert themselves inside of us where they can occupy and commandeer our will, our minds and our bodies. I find I sometimes have negative bizarre thoughts. I notice them and say, "No, Not my thought." If I don't claim the thoughts as my own, they don't influence me, and the thoughts leave. Have you noticed negative thoughts popping into your head? The thoughts we think are not our own, they are given us, but we don't have to accept them all without discernment.

TV shows, movies and magazines often normalize a set of morals and ideas that are dark, violent and disempowering, and subliminal messaging in TV and movies can influence us to buy, think or do things. (Binge watching episodes on Netflix for example.) Even though nothing can truly touch us as Consciousness, the presence of external images, opinions and ideas stresses our bodies, minds, emotions and spirits, compromising our sense of well being, our awareness of the Field of Love, our clarity, speed of thought, and some say it alters our DNA.[80] Untested technologies like 4G and 5G (and regular inoculations)[81] are unknown in their long-term effects on the human body, yet are increasingly influencing us 24/7.[82] 5G potentially covers the entire world, so there are fewer pure places free of such influence and intrusion upon Nature's purity.

---

[80] Molecular biology is being changed to digital biology, under the influence of technology and materials introduced into our environments. From an interview with Elana Freeland, author of *Geoengineered Transhumanism: How the Environment Has Been Weaponized By Chemicals, Electromagnetics, and Nanotechnology For Synthetic Biology*, https://rumble.com/v24rim4-geoengineered-transhumanism-elana-freeland-and-ana-mihalcea-md-phd.htm,

[81] "The vaccines recommended for children in 1972 was two doses, by the CDC schedule. Currently the CDC recommends 5fifty vaccine doses by age 6" —"Vaccination the Most Important Decision Parents Will Ever Make," The Weston A. Price Foundation. Www.WestonAPrice.org

[82] "5G Summit, Transcripts, 2020 Worldwide Call To Action," Hosted by Josh Del Sol and Sayer Ji

I don't watch TV, rarely listen to the radio and discontinued cable in the last century. When my son was nine or ten we would not use electricity on Sunday evenings. We would use candles, play games and read. I recall the sweetness of that feeling even now. It re-created a calmer deeper world. Choosing to curate the images we see and hear, and the environments, inputs and sounds that we tolerate in our homes and communities, can help us purify ourselves of negative outside influence. It's then easier to stay focused upon what we do wish to create. We can hear the gentle voice of Love within ourselves, the subtle prompts and impulses, as well as the call of the birds and the sound of the wind through the trees. It is easier when our environments are nature based, harmonious, nurturing and pure. Doing what we can, at biological, personal, community and subtle levels to safeguard healthy environments[83] makes good sense. It's an "ounce of prevention is worth a pound of cure" situation. Also, doing what we can to safeguard our schools and communities from wifi, cell towers, surveillance cameras and other intrusions is part of our important work at this time.

Our computers, phones and TV news have expanded our sphere of awareness of the world, sometimes accenting *what is wrong and not working.* This negatively influences our frequency. I mention some of these negative situations in this book, but only to awaken us to the urgent need to notice what's happening in the world, and to use these Laws to turn it around, in order to create what we *do* want. We need to have an incentive to turn this ship of humanity around. Not just for our own personal enjoyment and safety, but because *we are responsible for the future our children, grandchildren and the next seven generations that will inherit from our choices and actions.* Do you feel an urgency to protect our children's future? Once I had children I realized I needed to dig in and make this world a better place. We are all creators and stewards of this planet, and with teamwork and a shared focus, a positive future is

---

[83] See the 'Rays of Hope and reasons to prevail' section in the back of the book for information on Bau-biologie and BioGeometry, for help in purifying your living environments. In addition, Children that grow up in a wifi environment develop serious allergies in the second generation. -Dr Klinghardt inverview, on the 5G Summit.

possible. We can all become the foremothers and forefathers of Love's New Earth.

Our Wild Card—Who We Are

Don't despair. We are up to the task! As humans there is a power we embody that is our birthright. It is the power of *who we are*, both as Consciousness and Human Creators—as Divine Sparks of Infinity. We were gifted with the capacity and abilities to focus and create in the same way our Creator created us. That is, The Creator, the original Loving Creator, not the projected overlaid simulation creator (an idea David Icke brought forth in his book *The Dream*.)[84] The human body is a design miracle. We have the power to transcend what occurs in the world, to heal ourselves, to envision our ideas, create images in our minds, and build what we envision. We have the priceless abilities of our Creator and the free will to use them.

There are no limits to what is possible. In this mindset it is as easy to create a button as it is to create a castle. They are both the same in the manifest world, simply material ideas formed of Consciousness. One is not harder than the other to create. Lack and limitation need not sit in council with us in the creation of a New Earth. There is so much to do and there is so much to achieve, and none of it is beyond our reach. All is as it should be. Stretching and growth will and must occur to lift us and the systems we have created in life to the next level.

We can embody Love and see the people, situations and the world itself as within us. The capacity to create is ours. We just need to acknowledge it, use it and polish it up a bit. We have free will to align with Love and Nature's Laws. As we become conscious of what we have been aligning with other than Love, we can adjust our course and actively create and envision a world of Love, self-awareness, creativity and peace. We can also act directly upon the Earth by imagining what we wish to see, in

---

[84] Icke, David, (2023). *The Dream, The Extraordinary Revelation of Who We Are and Where We Are*, Derby U.K., Ickonic Publishing.

our mind's eye within ourselves. I have a globe that I use to project Light through my hands onto parts of the Earth that need it. I pop back and forth in perspective from my body's eyes to being so huge that the Earth is inside me or floating in front of me. In 1999 when I started channeling my spirit guides, they taught me to go out into space, look down on the Earth and notice energy blockages. I would creatively unblock them and it brought ease to the people living in those areas on the Earth. Wars occur in areas of Earth tension.[85] The tension in the Earth affects how the people interact upon it. We can do crazy wonderful things that seem absurdly impossible. We can do what feels right—and nature actually determines what happens as a result of our actions "on the ground." Can you imagine a wonderful outcome for humanity on Earth? Peace on Earth is possible.

> **A Vision board,** like a blueprint, uses images to call forth material reality, by creating a vision for the future using a large posterboard and a pile of magazines to clip photos and words from. The process is often playfully done, sometimes in a group where there is easy communication, support and anticipation, and where anything is possible, which is a perfect frequency to attract from. I have often pulled my vision boards out a year after making them to discover many things that had been created in my life were in the images on the board.[86] Sometimes they appeared even the next day. I remember a vision board a group of us made for the New Earth around 2017. It featured a lovely pregnant woman in a white dress, with the words *Nous sommes encore ici* (We are still here.). . . . Well, it seems the vision board did work; we are still here. And our New Earth baby is being born now!

---

[85] This was written of in *Be the Second Coming*, the author's second book.
[86] The movie, 'The Secret,' John Assaraf, http://thesecret-lawofattraction.net/teachers/john-assaraf/

We are impacting the world 24/7 whether we know it or not. If we picture our future is bright, we will influence it in that direction. This is the time for us to start using our inspired imagination consciously, with clarity and focus, staying true to *what we* do *want to create* is the key.

> The ripples of our pure Love expand infinitely, touching everyone and everything.

Most of us have not had the gift of life experiences or natural schooling to teach us these Creative Laws. Artificial schooling has changed our focus to what serves another master, rendering us ignorant of Nature's version of reading, writing and arithmetic—i.e., these four Laws and the knowledge of how to use them. A natural education would have taught us *who we are* and *how to navigate this world* using these Laws, while ensuring that our creations do no harm. And it would teach the importance of what we focus upon, community and self-responsibility. Instead of filling the students with a *product* of facts, dates and numbers, we would be teaching them the *process* of creation. We are so powerful that what we focus on and dwell upon grows in energy and materiality.

Group Creation

Joining together makes this process even more powerful.

> *"Alone we can do nothing, but together our wills fuse into something whose power is far beyond the power of its separate parts. By not being separate, the will of God is established in ours and as ours. This will is invincible because it is undivided."*
> — *A Course in Miracles, COA,* Ch 8, IV, 4, 2-4, P. 307

> *"The Union of the sonship is its protection."* — *A Course in Miracles, COA,* T-5.V.11:4[87]

---

[87] *A Course in Miracles* uses the word "sonship," and means all humans.

A shared human focus for deliberate intent and creation is very powerful and is an important key to creating a New Earth. Our world is a sentient amalgamation of all our creative actions, thoughts and energies. The power of shared focus is evident when random number generators placed around the world stop being random and become coherent during times when humanity is all focused with strong emotion upon the same thing. During 9/11[88] the numbers started becoming coherent *prior to* the flights hitting the World Trade Towers. It happened as well during the funeral of Princess Diana.[89] As more of us focus together on the same thing, our power to influence is strengthened. In Lynn McTaggart's book *The Power of Eight*,[90] she discovered that groups of eight people who focus healing energy towards another person who wanted healing can often heal that other person and are healed themselves. A coherent field is a healing field if there is a healing/love-based intent that activated or potentized it. As we join our focused thoughts together, we create a coherent field, our power to influence is multiplied. And this is the time, if there ever was one, to come together with a shared focus upon something we can all agree upon. Wouldn't that be something!

To fully realize the potential of a shared focus, it would be helpful to find a simple phrase that could create the New Earth, using the Law of Deliberate Intent, and that all humans might be able to stand behind, and enliven with their creative power? *How is this phrase for you?*

> ***Love as you would be Loved,***
> ***Give Light as you would like to be Lit***
> ***and to organize your Life to support such things for all beings.***

---

[88] Marc Newkirk pointed this out in one of his four talks on the "Scientific Evidence of Metaphysical Truths" in the Documentaries and other References section.

[89] Global Consciousness Project article on the random number generators during Princess Diana's funeral ceremony. https://noosphere.princeton.edu/ejap/diana/nelson_eJAP.htm

[90] *The Power of Eight*, a book by Lynn McTaggart, offers a system for gathering to create as a group of 8 people.

Imagine our world if all our actions were sourced in Love. We would *have to* end up with a loving peaceful world. Actions started from a lower consciousness—to *get even*, for example—end up creating something of that same lower frequency. With the above loving phrase in mind, the other day I passed a man carrying some heavy things—a gallon of milk and a twelve- pack of beer—on a beastly hot day. I saw him walking as I drove to do an errand, and he was still struggling along on a long empty stretch of road as I returned. So I turned around and picked him up. He didn't speak English and we awkwardly attempted to communicate, as I drove him in the direction he indicated. As I dropped him off and drove away, his joyful smile and prolonged wave of thanks (the universal language of Love and connection) across the busy street was certainly not lost on me and the many cars passing by in the center of Barre at rush hour. It was a moment outside of time, as his love created an opening beyond this physical world that rippled outward in all directions. The transcendent power of that moment mirrored the *power of the intent* I had to "Love as you would be Loved."

What if we all focused intently on creating Love's New Earth like a Labrador Retriever focuses on a tennis ball, or like professional athletes who do everything to support their goal of winning a game? Or like a contractor focuses on creating a house, or a director creates a highschool play, or the lead singer practices for her performance? For example, if our intent is good health, doing everything to support health, and *doing nothing that does not*. These Laws call our bluff. They respond with precision, but in their own way and timing. If we want something and don't support what we want with our frequency, thoughts, actions and words, we get what our frequency/actions/inactions *indicated* we wanted, not what we *said* we wanted. Nature's Laws *accrue*.

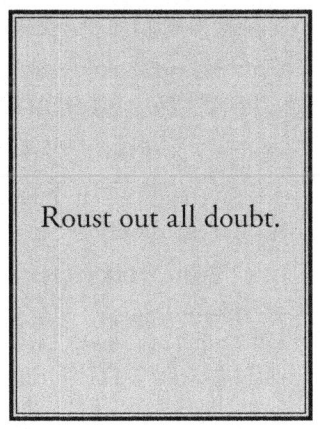

Roust out all doubt.

There is a mystery factor in all this because sometimes we act appropriately and still don't achieve our goal. So we can go back to the First Law (the great attractor) *adjust our frequency*, fine tune our image and we can also dial up the potent emotion of *having it already*.[91] (And, as Consciousness, we do have everything already!) The Laws don't understand negatives or qualifiers. They are an energetic language. So all creations are best created in the positive form. Focusing on lack brings more lack. *Wanting* creates more wanting. Instead, focus upon actually having the emotion that you would feel if you lived upon the kind of wonderful world you want—relief, peace, gratitude, generosity. We create physical things for the emotions that they cause in us. Feeling the emotion deeply, and artificially stimulating the creation of the emotion in our body, actually creates what we wanted all along. We have the power to skip the physical creation and just create the emotion we want within us. Our happiness is within us already, not sourced from the outer world. This is how our life on the New Earth can be here right now, already. This isn't just a sleight of hand. It is a potent creative tool that influences energy, matter and form.

Make Time To Create For Humanity

Making time to proactively create for our collective future either alone or in a group has massive potential to tip the balance in the direction of Love's New Earth. Allow yourself to daydream or meditate upon what it will be like, and share your visions. Perhaps you will be inspired, as you drive, to create positive outcomes for the people you see and transform the area you drive through into greater beauty in your imagination. Turn a homeless person into a happy, homed person; create gardens in empty city lots; remove phone bound eyes to smiling interactions with friends in your mind's eye.

We can accelerate our frequency and be more effective creators by attuning our inner core to the Oneness of Life and by allowing it to

---

[91] Check out *Emotional Transformation, Learn to Speak The Language of Creation*, a teaching audio CD that is free to download. https://www.freedomsart.com/emotional-transformation

become our guiding principle on Earth. As this unified focus saturates our Life and work, the frequency our physical body exists at accelerates. So it is an inner quest, for the truth of ourselves, which can be reflected outwardly with more potent creative results.

Don't be discouraged if the occurrences of the world continue along a negative trajectory for awhile. It's like turning off a ceiling fan: it keeps on turning even though there is no electricity moving its blades. There is a momentum in the Laws of Nature, and our positive world may not manifest instantly. Knowing the Laws can help us to be "steady-at the-helm" in times of dark, rough water. The dawn will eventually bring the light and the more peaceful seas of the New Earth.

Stillness

The largest trees have stayed still in place the longest. In stillness they have acquired great strength. They are visited, honored, named and Loved. Stillness has a power inherent within it that we mostly don't notice or actively draw upon, unless we meditate. In quiet stillness, we tap into our unchanging origin, the closest thing to who we Truly Are. Non-dual Consciousness is still and action-less. In stopping, we can sense the more subtle energies within and around us. Tom Brown, Jr.—known as "The Tracker"—shares that when we walk in the woods and see a deer, we have passed nine that we didn't see because they were so still and well camouflaged. Inner stillness is also an effective protective strategy. I surmise it can also render us invisible in a pinch. It is enough to be still. There are those of us in this world whose task is to just be still, hold our thoughts pure and keep our frequency high.

> *"Would you forever be a wanderer in search of peace? Faith in the eternal is always justified, for the eternal is forever kind, infinite in its patience, and wholly loving. It will accept you wholly and give you peace. But it can unite only*

with what already is at peace in you, immortal as itself."
— *A Course In Miracles*[92]

Stillness can mean non-movement or it can mean inner stillness as we move around. Stillness focuses our lens of perception toward both our inner and outer environments. After we are still for a while, peace can fully inhabit our bodies, so we can receive the information that our bodies are continually offering us, including information *beyond our five senses.* Stillness re-patterns our perceptions and environment. Think of the opportunity a stop sign gives when you are driving. It is placed where there are choices for where to go. When we stop for even a minute, our stop changes us and everything we are connected to. So, when confusion, anxiety or fear pop up, stop, become still. Take a moment. Feel what you feel without judgement. Observe it. Acknowledge it. And let it blow over. If it has negative thoughts attached to it say, "No, that is not my thought. That is not my reality." It may dissipate when *it* is ready, not when *you* are ready! In becoming still, we mimic the actionlessness of the rock, the ancient tree, the wisdom of the long-time meditator, the deer hiding in plain sight and the actionlessness of pure non-dual Consciousness, *perhaps correcting the unfolding direction of our Life.* In the stillness of the moment, time collapses, the past and future disappear, and the eternal present is all that is. It is a deep well of peace.

> "Stillness is a portal for accessing boundless electricity, developing healing technologies, expanding consciousness or simply finding peace of mind." -Kimberly Carter Gamble, *Thrive II, This is What it Takes.*

The diversions and distractions of the outer world can prevent us from being filled. When we are still and empty, we are more easily filled from on high. Our slowing down and stopping allows us to recharge

---

[92] *A Course In Miracles A Circle Of Atonement edition,* CH 19, IV, The attraction of Pain, 12:13:2-6.

the batteries of our divine Light—literally and figuratively this is so. Also a still form elicits stillness in those who come to it. Ben was "still" in his capacity to affect the world swirling around him when the gang cornered him. Our stillness reaches beyond the physical and calls forth higher levels of Light and opportunity. You might say it is the ground upon which Miracles may occur. The practice of stillness can help us all find the New Earth, where "do no harm" is the natural result of a whole society that knows its interconnectedness.

Navigating our lives in a body is a bit like playing an instrument: We can direct its volume, tempo, quality and expression. It is necessary to have the loud drums and trumpets, and also the very quiet and subtle instruments that support all others without calling attention to themselves. *"We are cobbling together the human orchestra of light to bring to this Earth the world of humanity as one family, the world of peace There is a place for everyone to be who they are, to share their gifts, to love one another, to have shelter and food."*[93]

---

[93] From the Dark and Stormy Night booklet, by the Author, it is Jesus' voice .https://www.freedomsart.com/offerings

CH IV THE PANDEMIC BEGAN

*If everything around seems dark, look again,
you may be the light. - Rumi*

These were times of rough water. *"It was a dark and stormy night on planet Earth"*[94] when it was announced that there was a sickness that was spreading from Wuhan China, and officials predicted its arrival in the USA. It then crept and jumped its way across the country on airplanes, trains and through all variety of human interactions. I mention the pandemic to show where we were as a human family in 2020, because it radically changed the world. I wanted to explain why we need to intentionally create a New Earth, for future readers who didn't live through these times to know how radically life changed. This pandemic event set the stage for our world's transformation to begin. In birthing terms, labor began, we got squeezed.

We all went from living normally, which meant freedom to travel where we wanted, freedom to see who we wanted, freedom to choose the medicines that work for us and as our doctor saw fit to suggest, to the national and state governments forcing people to shut their stores and businesses and being told to stay home. All of a sudden the government claimed oversight of medicine, religious gatherings, education and home life. The governmental leaders, medical professionals and the Center for Disease Control were trying to figure out how to keep the sickness from

---

[94] From the Dark and Stormy Night booklet, by the Author, it is Jesus' voice.

spreading. First they said masks were useless, then they were required and enforced almost everywhere in public. I sewed fabric masks like some others did and gave them to the local hospital early on, when there were none available to buy. With masks required in public places, speaking was muffled, words were unintelligible and it was hardly worth the effort to interact. You couldn't tell if someone was smiling.

"Social distancing" directed people to stay six feet apart,[95] with stickers saying "stand here" on the floor at the checkout counters in stores. The elderly in nursing homes were confined to their rooms and many died alone, heartbreakingly isolated from their families that were not allowed to visit. "Contact tracing" used cell phone locations: if you were in the proximity of someone discovered to be sick with Covid-19, you were asked to test or quarantine yourself. Covid testing was centralized. They created locations where one would drive up to a white tent and a highly protected nurse with head, face, arm and hand coverings, would stick a swab way up your nose and twirl it. (I had it done once.) People would isolate themselves in their homes for five days to two weeks if they tested positive, sometimes even without any symptoms. Later on at-home tests became available. The Center for Disease Control banned Ivermectin[96] and determined that Resveratrol was to be what treated Covid-19 patients—an across-the-board solution, which in the area of medicine is a very unusual way to treat patients, as though they all need the same medical treatment.

Parks, beaches, pools and public spaces were closed. In some places when people ignored the outdoor bans, they were violently removed by police. Schools all went to remote learning, sending students home from

---

[95] Dr. Anthony Faucci, a key figure in the pandemic plan for the US Government, said recently to a Congressional Committee that the 6 foot rule " sort of just appeared" and was "not likely based on scientific data." https://www.msn.com/en-us/health/medical/phony-fauci-fesses-up-on-fake-science-and-covid-flim-flam/ar-AA1mUBaL

[96] A promising medication in treating the Covid-19 virus, used by doctors successfully in the first weeks of the pandemic, that cost 17 cents a dose and was effective and available over the counter.

college, high school, elementary schools and younger, to sit alone in front of a computer for classes (no tuition was refunded). Some families spent more meaningful time and ate meals together and had time to re-connect. Many re-evaluated their life choices, and later moved to less stressful jobs and locations. There were delays and shortages in getting supplies and the general commodities of modern life. It wasn't unusual to see empty shelves in grocery stores (a rare sight prior to that time). Strangely, toilet paper was in high demand and sold out within hours of restocking it. Amazon and other online stores did a bang-up business. Personal income was slowed or stopped completely for some. The federal government, under President Donald Trump, sent out economic stimulus checks for $1,400 to all Americans in March of 2020, and later on, checks were sent twice more with lesser amounts. Isolation set in as the months dragged on. Some people were stranded in foreign countries, stuck in hotel rooms, unable to return home or move about. Zoom, the internet meeting facilitation company, became a household word as the interactions of life went online. Meetings, parties, reunions and even funerals were held via Zoom. There were no real parties.

A vaccine was talked about and many pharmaceutical labs were hastily working to bring one to the market. President Trump called it Operation Warp Speed. A normal vaccine takes seven to ten years to create. Officials assured the public that the vaccine wouldn't become mandatory, and many people were eager to receive it. There was an extensive public relations campaign, glorifying the willingness of movie stars, politicians and other well-known people to take the vaccine.[97] It was called a "vaccine" but it did not prevent your getting the illness, just made the symptoms less extreme. A Vaccine Passport was introduced for a time, limiting access to higher and continuing education, dance and art classes, concerts, stores and travel for the "unvaccinated" or

---

[97] From *Died Suddenly,* a documentary, at the 30 minute mark, https://www.diedsuddenly.info/, and also in David Martin's speech to the Weston A Price Foundation, https://www.bitchute.com/video/fHhniBm4cyiM/ towards the end, he identifies Fors Marsh as the US company involved in this propaganda campaign calling them "the COVID privateers."

those who hadn't taken the full quota of recommended shots. (As of 2023 the *experimental* "vaccine" is recommended for babies as young as 6 months old.)

It's No Time to be Alone

As the lockdown was unfolding in March 2020, I invited my friend Ben to come and live in my guest room while he was renovating his house, saying that "This is no time to be alone." Ben was part of the wave of love and the radical lifestyle in the 60s and never sold out to the traditional system. He was aware of the limitations and compromises that had been made to our Constitutional freedoms and was suspicious from the start of the pandemic, having been part of a group working to bring the government back to a true Republic. On the internet constantly, Ben discovered an interview titled "A Call to Humanity"[98] that caught his attention. "Hey, come take a look at this." And there on a YouTube video was a diminutive woman with hair shaved short like a Buddhist Nun's, with a refined British accent, being interviewed by Stephen and Theresa,[99] a young American couple. She had a unique grasp of the playbook of what is happening on Earth because, she said, she had been in this situation before on other planets. She said she carries the frequency codes for success in this situation that we now face. Her name is "Oracle Girl," and she holds the frequency of "Embodying more Love on this planet."[100]

Her perspective was unique, evolved and seemed timeless. She used her own vocabulary, not religious, spiritual or scientific, and was hopeful and down-to-Earth. Since then, her expansive vision has helped me

---

[98] https://www.oraclegirl.org/library/a-call-to-humanity
[99] Stephen and Theresa can be found on Ownstream, "Ownstream is a private, high frequency, censorship-free online community and resource hub designed to gather, support and organize an awakened community in these dynamic and changing times, and assist in positive planetary transformation.' https://ownstream.mn.co/landing?from=https%3A%2F%2Fownstream.mn.co%2Fposts%2Fmanaging-your-subscription-and-leaving-the-network
[100] https://www.oraclegirl.org

immensely to make sense of the world that has been fully turned upside-down. I started listening to her twice a week "Reboot"[101] recordings that are part of the "Purification Space."[102] Oracle Girl's recordings helped me to move beyond the increasing fear I felt around the world pandemic situation. Fear, not from the illness outright, but from the worldwide push for control of our bodies, minds and lives, and the polarization of the people, fueled by the media. So much hope was being put on the "experimental vaccines" that those who were not vaccinated were labeled as "anti-vaxers," "conspiracy theorists" and troublemakers. "Vaccine hesitancy" actually became a thing that the news talked about eradicating. Oracle Girl mentioned the Nuremberg Code,[103] an international code of ethics put in place after World War II which states that no one can be forced to participate in medical experiments without their full awareness and consent, a code that many people were and still are conspicuously unaware of. It was a great relief to know about it since the "vaccines" were experimental, untested, and used mRNA (messenger ribonucleic acid) technology, a type of vaccine technology that had never previously been used successfully *because of its longterm effects*.[104] Little did I know while seeing that first interview how important Oracle Girl's recordings would become to me. They became a lifeline of sanity as the pandemic plan rolled out.

---

[101] https://www.oraclegirl.org/event/reboot-group

[102] https://www.oraclegirl.org/glossary, definition of Purification is in the Appendix.

[103] The Nuremberg Code is listed in the Appendix, it is worth reading.

[104] No mRNA vaccine had ever been made available before because, as I recall (and can no longer find a link to), when mRNA vaccine was used in a study with ferrets, the injection helped the immune system of the ferrets battle against the targeted contagion, but was ineffective with other immune challenges later on. Their immune system had become trained to only deal with the one thing, and so when the ferrets were beyond the threat that the mRNA injection had targeted, and were re-introduced into a natural environment, with other stresses upon their immune systems "most of the lab animals died." That background info on mRNA vaccines was never shared with people evaluating whether to get the inoculation, and there was outright coercion and incentivizing to receive the experimental mRNA vaccine shot. I later found a reference to this in *A Mom's Guide to the COVID Shot* by Christiane Northrup, M.D.

How Could This Be?

A hotel security camera recorded a conference that enacted a *dry run of the official response* to Covid-19 pandemic, six months *before* it all happened. It was called *Event 201, A Global Pandemic Exercise*,[105] and the scenario drilled included TV news and press conferences announcing shortages, promoting a vaccine, and repeating that the vaccine was the only solution to getting back to normal and more. The event drilled situations which then did happen, down to the last detail. (The event was co-sponsored by the Bill and Melinda Gates[106] Foundation.) I realized that the entire official Covid-19 response had been planned, scripted and choreographed ahead of time. The intention behind it appeared to be to manipulate public opinion, divide people into separate camps and to engender fear in order to create a docile, obedient populace, willing to be vaccinated[107] and follow rules. The conference was documented in *Plandemic 2, InDOCTORnation*.[108]

I had to seriously question the official pandemic story line and re-assess the true intentions and benevolence of the US government, pharmaceutical corporations, media and other public officials. I was never interested in conspiracy theories; they seemed like unproductive lines of thought because (I thought) they could not be proven. I have always been an optimist and careful of where I put my attention, having studied the Laws of Creation for many years. But this scripted evidence from before the illness even existed, and before it was made public, and which looked exactly like what occurred during the pandemic,

---

[105] https://rumble.com/v1mxliy-plandemic-2-indoctornation-full-documentary.html, The event was hosted by the Bill and Melinda Gates Foundation, The World Economic Forum and the John Hopkins Center for Health and Security.

[106] Bill Gates has said that vaccines are the best (financially lucrative) investments he's ever made.

[107] In the book *Vax Unvax, Let The Science Speak*, by Robert F Kennedy Jr, and Brian Hooker, The Vaccine Adverse Event Reporting VAERS system, reported over 33,000 deaths, from the Covid-19 Vaccine, and many permanent injuries.

[108] *Plandemic 2: InDOCTORnation*, a documentary, https://www.bitchute.com/video/ZFjRALF5nkHd/

> Discernment is an important skill. Tune in and ask yourself, how do I feel and what do I think about this? Who stands to gain? Does it make sense? What would George Washington think?

was horrifying and could not be ignored. It later became evident that many heads of government[109] that were spearheading the pandemic response were being manipulated by a central money-driven force. Governments, hospitals, schools, colleges and other organizations were evidently given significant money to align with and enforce the centralized Covid-19 Pandemic plan. In three months during the spring of 2020 when the pandemic was unfolding, the five richest men in the world increased their wealth by 26%.[110] As I learned more, I discovered a global plan to create a centralized world government of top-down control called The Great Reset, spearheaded by the World Economic Forum, United Nations, World Health Organization, global corporations and other "stakeholders." Under their plan, nothing would be individually owned[111] as of 2030. Humanity was scheduled to be reduced in its freedoms, confined, rationed and equalized, living in "smart cities" with a small radius of ability to travel. Thus it was a drastic, severe and police-enforced change being planned and rehearsed, that was "determined" (a word used repeatedly in the WEF documents) to encompass all humanity and all countries, imposed from a central, unelected source that claimed power for itself, all by itself, over the

---

[109] President Biden, (then) 'Prince' Charles, and other leaders are all seen repeating the same phrase "build back better." In *Plandemic 3*, the great "opportunity" is shown at minute 16, in the documentary, where heads of state are repeating the script in synchrony. https://plandemicseries.com/watch-the-great-awakening-movie/

[110] Cummins, Ronnie, pg 179 footnote, in The book *The Truth About COVID-19, Exposing The Great Reset, Lockdowns, Vaccine Passports, and the New Normal*, by Dr. Joseph Mercola and Ronnie Cummins,

[111] The World Economic Forum website's 10 points, includes "you will own nothing and you will be happy." The video from 2016 is no longer available on line. "Who owns the data owns the future." https://plandemicseries.com/watch-the-great-awakening-movie/

entire world. It appears—rather convincingly when you look at the evidence[112]—as though a world takeover is being attempted. In the documentary *Plandemic 3*, one of the World Economic Forum's Advisors said,

> "*Science is replacing evolution by intelligent design, not the intelligent design of some God above the clouds, but our intelligent design, and the intelligent design of our clouds, the IBM cloud, the Microsoft cloud, these are the new driving forces of evolution. We have the technology to hack human beings on a massive scale, and by this I mean,* **if you have enough data and enough computing power, then you can understand people better than they understand themselves, and then you can manipulate them in ways that were previously impossible.** [emphasis added] *You know, the whole idea that humans have a soul and free will, that is over.*"[113]
> —Yuval Noah Harari, Advisor, World Economic Forum

Let that sink in. Let that sink in. The "data" he mentioned is gathered from surveillance cameras and satellites, phone conversations and cameras, social media posts, emails, credit card records, and financial records, etc., and the computing power comes from 5G and Artificial Intelligence (AI). Technologies of surveillance are far more advanced

---

[112] See *Plandemic2 InDOCTORnation*, https://plandemicseries.com/watch-the-great-awakening-movie/; David Martin's speech entitled: Weaponization of Coronavirus: When Nature is Conscripted to Harm, at the Weston A Price Foundation https://www.bitchute.com/video/fHhniBm4cyiM/(highly recommended); The Trojan Horse of the Digital Panopticon, https://www.youtube.com/watch?v=p1i3k-zrYWE; and the movie thrive 2 by Foster and Kimberly Gamble _https://www.youtube.com/watch?v=nq2MCxXn3vg; Del Bigtree, and Coin Bureau, with Guy https://www.youtube.com/watch?v=0wxY1sojA6A; Additional documentaries are listed in the Documentaries and other Reference Materials section.

[113] *Plandemic 3* documentary, minute 23. https://plandemicseries.com/watch-the-great-awakening-movie/

than most of us realize. A former Navy employee I met said that each of our unique brain signatures can be identified from space.

A vast wealth redistribution is also planned. *The Great Taking*, a documentary and a book by David Rogers Webb, outlines how our homes, land, cars, stocks, bonds—things we have paid for with our own money—are *not in fact legally ours*.[114] They are owned by "the protected class" and can be taken without our consent or recourse. Moving us into Smart Cities is their plan. The WEF[115] and their hundreds of corporate and business partners will provide everything we need in life, that we use daily and take for granted and will become a *"service."*[116] If they don't like how we think or what we do, they can refuse or deny us basic necessities and withhold our money. This plan is manipulating, controlling and horrifying. The more I learned, the more troubled I became, because unless someone was aware of the nefarious intent of the global plan, they could easily fall for their politically correct rhetoric of so-called green initiatives, sustainable practices, global warming,[117] social justice and equality. These initiatives have sold the dark plan

---

[114] The book *The Great Taking,* on page 11 says, "The absolute priority claim of secured creditors to pooled client securities has been upheld by the courts." This is a tiny piece of a monumental discovery, that our ownership has been eroded. Our stocks, cars, houses and more can be taken free of payment (FoP).

[115] Claus Schwab, the former head of WEF said, "China is a role model for many countries. We have to go one step further to a systemic transformation of the world." "Artificial Intelligence, the metaverse, synthetic biology, our life ten years from now will be completely different, and who masters those technologies will be master of the world." From https://plandemicseries.com/watch-the-great-awakening-movie/ at the 23 minute mark,

[116] Mercola, Dr. Joseph, pg 47 footnote, in *The book The Truth About COVID-19 Exposing The Great Reset, Lockdowns, Vaccine Passports, and the New Normal*, by Dr. Joseph Mercola and Ronnie Cummins, (2021), White River Junction VT, Chelsea Green Publishing. Their footnote indicates this is from World Health Organization and World Economic Forum, "Preventing Noncommunicable Disease in the Workplace Through Diet and Physical Activity." World Health Organization, 2008,

[117] Patrick Moore, Greenpeace Co-Founder's talk entitled "Why CO_2 Is Not the Enemy They Want You to Believe." Available on YouTube : https://www.youtube.com/watch?v=TclmRoTGsO4

to people as a logical and necessary solution for global problems (that they defined and elected themselves to solve). The Great Reset and its sinister end-goal is complete control of all humanity and the world under the guise of saving us all. Their scripted words and phrases have been repeated and reinforced so often, they have become solidified, normalized and acceptable, and impenetrable to discussion, questioning or challenge. Logic and discourse were steamrolled and squelched.

The choreography of the globalist control agenda is widespread, impeccable, convincing and deadly. Many have innocently fallen into step with its mandates, dictates, and clever social programming and thus have become its deputies. Some have been actively trained in this social programming methodology by The World Economic Forum in their Young Global Leaders program. The global program already has *regional offices* that are working to put this plan into place at the local level.[118]

Mass Formation Psychosis

It was a year later that the phenomenon of Mass Formation Psychosis was brought to light by Matias Desmet. It is the process of creating the mental rigidity and impenetrability that so many people who were plugged into the mainstream media have been exhibiting. A hypnosis occurs when there are certain preconditions:

- When people are de-coupled from each other and fragmented.
- When whatever happens just doesn't make sense.
- When there is free floating anxiety that is chronic.
- When there is discontent, and there is a single point of focus that the population is focused upon and obsessed about. Once this happens, the people lose their capacity to think, and can be actively managed psychologically.

---

[118] Rosa Koire's talk about Agenda 21, https://m.youtube.com/watch?v=H-qLUQlmBk4

- A leader then steps in and can manage (solve) the situation, claiming anything they want to, and the crowd will believe it.
- Any outside dissenters must be attacked, a common enemy is required.

During the pandemic those who did not choose to take the experimental inoculation became the common enemy, dividing married couples, parents and children, siblings, lifelong friends, employees and employers, and more. Mass Formation Psychosis was the same process that was used by Hitler in Nazi Germany to coalesce the German people behind his agenda.

What can be done in this type of situation to awaken those hypnotized? The only solution according to Mattias Desmet is to substitute the fear for a greater threat. So as the fear of Covid-19 has dwindled with time, it has been replaced with the fear of global warming by the global powers, in order to maintain the hypnosis and their control.

It was heartbreaking to discover the mechanism of this psychosis. Many of us who were concerned about the safety of the vaccine, feared for the lives of those who were taking it, and had been attempting to communicate this concern to our families and friends who simply couldn't and wouldn't listen. Trying to reach people who couldn't hear was frustrating, exhausting and terrifying. It was like watching someone you love back off a cliff. After realizing that there was no hope of reaching them anymore, I finally just stopped trying. It was a huge relief and the greatest sadness at the same time.

Interestingly, most people are still unaware of Mass Formation Psychosis, and The Great Reset—with its radical plan for humanity scheduled to take place in just a few short years—because the globalists have done such a thorough job of keeping the bigger plan of global control hidden or disguised behind socially- and politically-correct fences that cannot be debated because of the Mass Formation Psychosis suffered by a vast sector of the population.

The foundation stone for the plan for control of humanity is Global Warming. The pandemic was just an important first exercise. Global Warming is being blamed upon humanity, and the plan to rectify its impact includes draconian changes in how we live as dictated by the Great Reset designers.

> Patrick Moore, Greenpeace Co-Founder's talk entitled *Why CO_2 is not the Enemy they Want you to Believe* offers evidence that atmospheric *carbon levels don't cause temperature increases* on Earth; it is the other way around. *The increasing temperature on Earth is causing the increase in CO_2* levels. In addition Marc Newkirk said that *the temperature is rising on all the planets* in our solar system, not just on the Earth. Carbon is a huge aid to plant growth. Moore looks at millions of years of data to bring carbon's present levels into perspective. It is lower now than it has been at many times in the Earth's past. This kind of information ought to be factored into the discussion on the global plan for dealing with whatever effects we are experiencing and predicting on Earth.

The Global Plan is all woven together with the global roll out of 5G,[119] artificial intelligence (AI), central bank digital currencies (CBDC), digital IDs tied to our biometric data[120] (images of our face, body and how we walk), and regular vaccines and booster shots.[121] The Global

---

[119] 5G, requires thousands of satellites in the lower atmosphere, and antennae in highly populated areas every 300 meters or so. It emits untested-on-humans, microwave frequency bands. Substantial scientific evidence indicates its harm to humans. No studies support its safety. The FCC has admitted no testing has been done on it, and yet licensing of corporations to install its infrastructure is continuing to be built out now.

[120] https://www.biometricupdate.com/ A resource for what is happening along this front.

[121] A vaccine is a bit of the offending material that renders the recipient immune to getting the ailment. The Covid-19 "vaccine" was a misnomer. It never claimed to

Plan also includes the programming of humanity to become part of technology, both externally and internally. External technologies include cellphones, handheld devices, ear buds, watches, etc. Internal technologies include body chips installed under the skin, and other technologies that interact biologically at a more intimate level. mRNA technology (first deployed experimentally in the Covid-19 "vax") as a delivery system may have possible benefits, but it also could alter us on a very fundamental basis. We don't know what it may do to human genetics over time, yet it has been injected worldwide in vast doses. Other substances, such as graphene oxide[122] and nanoparticles may be inhaled, ingested and injected. These can self-form into wire-like segments. They potentially can become like electronically controllable hardware inside the body. (The wire-like segments may be the cause of the mysterious blood clots, heart attacks and strokes affecting many.) Humans combined with machines become transhuman and this could bring some very negative outcomes, as humans can then be remotely controlled and perhaps incited to violence, suicide or other behavioral extremes, such as the mass shootings in the schools and stores. One of the emotional symptoms of taking the vaccine is becoming more placid and less vibrant (a symptom I personally observed), and is a useful trait in a controllable populace.

Evidently Rudolph Steiner saw this coming:

> *In the future, we will eliminate the soul with medicine. Under the pretext of a "healthy point of view," there will be a vaccine, by which the human body will be treated as soon as possible, directly at birth, so that the human*

---

make the recipient immune to the Covid-19 infection and used mRNA, a system, *never used successfully before*; in animal trials, the animals all died when they were reintroduced to the natural stresses of a normal environment.

[122] Graphene Oxide poisoning provides the Covid-19 symptoms. It has been found in masks, swabs for Covid-tests, and in vaccines: *Pfizer, Astrazeneca, Moderna and Janssen.* https://www.orwell.city/2021/07/COMUSAV-CONUVIVE.html this English speaking source reported on the findings from "La Quinta Columna" in Argentina.

being cannot develop the thought of the existence of soul and Spirit.

To materialistic doctors, will be entrusted the task of removing the soul of humanity. As today, people are vaccinated against this disease or that disease, so in the future, children will be vaccinated with a substance that can be produced precisely in such a way that people, thanks to this vaccination, will be immune to being subjected to the "madness" of spiritual life.

He would be extremely smart, but he would not develop a conscience, and that is the true goal of some materialistic circles. With such a vaccine, you can easily make the etheric body loose in the physical body. Once the etheric body is detached, the relationship between the universe and the etheric body would become extremely unstable, and man would become an automaton, for the physical body of man must be polished on this Earth by Spiritual will.

So the vaccine becomes a kind of arymanique [negative satanic] *force; man can no longer get rid of a given materialistic feeling. He becomes materialistic of constitution and can no longer rise to the spiritual.*

—Rudolph Steiner (1861-1925)[123]

This correlates chillingly with the World Economic Forum's Advisor's statement: ". . . you know the whole idea of humans having a soul and free will, that is over." No dissent or discussion about the experimental vaccine's stated safety or efficacy was even allowed. It was publicly promoted everywhere as "safe and effective." The voices of reason, sanity, logic and science were censored and prevented from reaching the public. Highly qualified doctors, nurses, scientists, researchers—many

---

[123] https://www.ahlcglobal.com/blog/seeing-through-the-veil/soul-separation-via-vyroos-vax

leading experts in their fields—were not interviewed on mainstream outlets and were censored, ignored, slandered, accused of spreading "disinformation" (a very Orwellian sounding label), and their scientific research papers were removed from online access and from premier scientific journals like *Nature*.[124] Social media platforms, YouTube and Facebook, censored and de-platformed them and others who shared similar facts and information. Anyone who questioned or countered the morality, science and logic of the (unified) pandemic response was vulnerable to receive such treatment. Freedom of speech and freedom to gather were eliminated. The mind washing was complete as many people supported such measures. The truckers in Canada who peacefully protested had their bank accounts frozen or closed, as has happened as well in the US.[125] Many healthy people have died or were permanently injured from the vaccine.[126] By law the vaccine manufacturers are not liable for any damage, death or injury to the public that their vaccines cause. As of this writing in late 2023 aggressive cancers and "unexplained deaths" have skyrocketed[127] in the 18-49 year old range. A friend who works in a Boston hospital said that there are many more deaths than usual occurring, and the hospital is in a constant and unsustainable state of emergency.

---

[124] *Plandemic* documentary

[125] David Martin's mentioned his company's bank accounts were frozen in his speech to the Weston A. Price Foundation, and Dr Mercola's, and other working for him, had their bank accounts frozen, as well.

[126] VAERS, the Vaccine Adverse Event Reporting System, a government organization: https://vaers.hhs.gov/, reported 33,000 associated deaths with the vaccine. I was unable to verify this number when I entered Covid-19 into the search bar. The following message appeared: "Error 403 – Forbidden. The web app you have attempted to reach has blocked your access." There are many videos online of young athletes suddenly keeling over on the field, not even attempting to protect themselves from falling, and many young people now have myocarditis, permanent damage to the heart and heart attacks..

[127] A 40% increase. "US Life Insurance agencies report an overwhelming and unexplainable increase in all-cause deaths in 18-49 year olds," spoken by a news announcer in the *Died Suddenly* documentary. https://rumble.com/v1wac7i-world-premier-died-suddenly.html

In 2020 however, you would never know there was a "pandemic," some people were sick, and it took a long time to recover but there weren't bodies in the streets. Most of the people who died were elderly or sick with other ailments already. The forces behind this whole situation were frantic to maintain fear by having lots of deaths associated with the illness. Fear is an excellent medium for seizing and holding on to control. John O'Looney, a British funeral director, posted a call with his fellow funeral directors wherein they agreed that *there were no more dead bodies than normal.*[128] As the *statistical* deaths from Covid-19 *spiked*, the deaths from cancer and heart disease *dipped*. People who died from multiple causes were labeled as Covid-19 deaths, inflating the statistics and the actual death numbers from Covid-19 alone. Doctors were instructed to name Covid-19 as the cause of death, *in any death,* in order for the hospital to receive more Covid-19 payment money. Hospitals received $13,000 for a covid Intensive Care Unit (ICU) patient, and $39,000 for a Covid-19 death. A chilling incentive and a great way to inflate the death statistics and keep fear levels high. A woman in Connecticut whose husband died in a motorcycle accident received the death certificate which listed Covid-19 as the cause. There is about a 99% chance of recovery from Covid-19 for all ages under sixty.

A Community Forms

Such turmoil in the world can be destabilizing, it tests our ability to stay centered and focused on what we do want. Through the online *Ownstream*[129] platform's network, I met some high frequency women as concerned about the world situation and governments overstepping

---

[128] The oridiginal video I mentioned was censored and removed. A search uncovered this one. https://archive.org/details/exh-43, John O' Looney. Put the following in the search bar if the link doesn't work: Archive/ 43 Funeral Doctor Reveals Mass Murder By Government, John O' Looney. 35 Minutes long, and well worth a watch. He also said the death rate increased hugely when the vaccinations began, in all age categories.

[129] The Ownstream Website, https://ownstream. mn.co/landing?from=https%3A%2F%2Fownstream. mn.co%2Fposts%2F19696839%3Fnotification_id%3D2155922229

their authority as I was. After Ben moved back into his newly renovated house after six months, my friend Eileen sold her house and moved into mine. A few months later, Veronica sold hers and joined us. Their presence in my life was comforting, grounding and made the pandemic situation a lot more fun. We kept each other sane in a world turned upside down... the safe and benevolent world, was no longer. It was a first step towards creating a community. Ironically, the pandemic brought us all more friends than we had ever had, as the black sheep of the world happily found each other!

> Your body's subtle messages, are valuable for navigating these times.

The three of us created a document of intention, signed it, and bought a rattletrap farmhouse in western Massachusetts in February of 2022. It needed remediation for mold and vermiculite, as well as some new windows, appliances, paint and flooring. Amazingly, we found a contractor and his team who were available to do the work. Many contractors had been booked solid for a year during the pandemic, with all the household changes people wanted to make as they worked from home and spent more time there. Eileen planted an orchard first thing, a symbolic investment in the land, the future and food to share. A large garden, a well, a propane tank, a beautiful solar-controlled greenhouse and a chicken coop rounded out our budding homestead. Later, Veronica's skilled decorator's eye and stockpile of furniture turned it into a cozy home.

It wasn't always easy, as the three of us had to adjust, accommodate and compromise in response to each other's needs, expectations and ways of doing things. All three of us were used to being queens in our own homes. It brought up our emotional patterns (running away, becoming a victim, projecting our stuff onto others) for us to see and acknowledge. It was certainly a pressure cooker. In normal times, we might have disbanded. The pressure of the world around us, its potential sinister nature and instability, kept us together as much as our joy in each other's company, our shared values, and the fun and communion we experienced. We laughed a lot and the fact that we were all from large families helped us roll with the punches. We were listening to Oracle Girl's twice a week "Reboot"[130] recordings, and so our conversations were peppered with the recording topics. By hearing Oracle Girl share ahead of time her frequency perspective on what was happening and the future potentialities of what might happen on the world stage...we moved beyond the fear of it, a very uncomfortable but much-needed process. In community, it was a hopeful time as we were creating a new way of living together for ourselves, and we were an inspiration to friends wishing for community also. We trusted that our path forward was together, and that our inner compasses knew the way to go. We stayed positive, hoping for the best while preparing for the worst.

I realized it was time to move when I just found myself packing things up. As Eileen and Veronica and I were looking for a house to buy together to create a community, we all just kept going in the same direction. So we *trust* that we are here at this time on Earth for a reason, we are moving forward together, each with our unique skills and talents, trusting that we are where we need to be in each and every moment, and fulfilling the roles we came to play. The time was so stressful that remembering that we are One Consciousness and exist in a Field of Love has been challenging to say the least! These times are giving us a fabulous opportunity to get out of our own way!

Now What?

The pressure of these times is helping us all to evolve and mature in a way that times of ease would never offer. Many small businesses were forced out of business during the pandemic shutdown, further

> The time for going it alone is over, join together with family and friends regularly, talk about how you can help each other.

---

[130] https://www.oraclegirl.org/event/reboot-group

condensing ownership of daily services and products into the hands of large global corporations. We, and many people all over the world who have awakened to this situation, are working to awaken others and become more responsible for ourselves, more independent of the corporate systems that control food, water, money and life's necessities, systems that have become less reliable and seemingly weaponized.[131] We are making the best of this intense time of radical change that is also pregnant with possibility for creating a more loving and just way of living upon the Earth. But first we've got to get past the shock, fear and horror of discovering this global plan.

John Root's Building Community:

People are attracted to come together to form a community by an aim that resonates with their heartfelt life purpose. The word *community* is made up of two root meanings: *co-* is "together," and *munus* (Latin) is "gift." So community means "our together gifts."

A general aim for creating a self-governing community would be some version of creating the society we know in our hearts is possible, or creating the society to benefit everyone. Everyone is perfect in their essential being, and everyone is handicapped in bringing that perfection to expression. This understanding allows us to recognize and further each other's initiatives and recognize and compensate for each other's disabilities.

To do this in a way that is socially constructive:

- we share our biographies, answering the question *"What is my life's purpose?"*

---

[131] There is a war on farmers, food, organic, biodynamic and other diversity based systems that don't require vast chemical inputs. Fake food, made in laboratories is being promoted as the solution to Global Warming. It is misguided and devious. Evidently spinach and lettuce are being developed that introduce the mRNA material into you if you eat it. It is being test marketed in Ontario, Canada. Insects are being promoted as food.

- followed by each sharing *what we feel we have to do with each other, how my interests and talents relate to each of the other's purposes.*
- When there is a sense that we have a good understanding of and appreciation for each of us, and a shared sense of what we have to do with each other, we can answer the question: *"What do we desire and how would we like the world to be?"*
  - → This question may be answered in general terms such as *"I desire to be free to pursue the transcendent purpose I feel called to serve, autonomously and with the ongoing opportunities to be ever better at doing it.*
  - → *I desire to live in a society based on our common sense of justice, and I desire to collaborate with others to provide everything that we need and desire to create a community in which we each can say: 'The community is as I desire it to be and I am diligently doing my part to make it so.'"*
- And we can then delve into the practicalities of accomplishing it.

Self-governing communities do not vote because voting creates winners and losers. We gather in small circles with specific aims, we hear from everyone in turn, around the circle, and we welcome objections because they contain valuable information, and we come up with criteria for evaluating our proposal and the timeframe when it will be evaluated. We may then consent to it as "good enough for now and safe enough to try." We are always selecting the best person for every role, and always with evaluation criteria and term.

- *When we are a large enough community of largely autonomous circles we implement community-created credit (currency) in which everyone has the right to the capital their capacities warrant, with no debt and no interest.*

—John G Root Jr, Just Abundance, Inc.: "Community-Created Credit and Sociocracy, shift the paradigm" http://www.justabundance.org/

CH V FREEDOM FROM FEAR

Fear is the cheapest room in the house.
I would like to see you living in better conditions. — Hafiz [132]

Miracles Need Freedom from Fear

> *"Nothing is gained by frightening yourself, and it's very destructive. Miracles need freedom from fear. Part of their Atonement value involves that very freedom."*

> — Miracle Principle 24[133]

The global plan is terrifying and fearful. It is enough to knock us all out of our centered wholeness and perspective into separation from ourselves, eachother and our true power. The mention of fear as a danger to our *Atonement*—or our *at-one-ment*—and a danger to knowing ourselves as whole, struck me because from the very moment it was announced, the pandemic has been one massive choreographed fear campaign in a brazen and perhaps brilliant attempt at severing the innate power of humans from themselves. Fear, like a scalpel, removes our own power from us by disconnecting us from ourselves—our Whole Self and our internal guidance. Freedom from fear is a key to transcending the global

---

[132] Jalāl al-Dīn Muhammad Rūmī the 13th-century Persian poet and mystic. His legacy includes beautiful poetry and the whirling dervishes.
[133] *A Course In Miracles,* A book dictated by Jesus to Helen Schucman in New York City in the mid 1960's.

plan, which is why fear is a key tool being used to attempt to control and undermine us. It turns off our innate inner sense of security and moves us to search outwardly for security instead. Those crafting the global plan know and use this, providing "up-to-date information" and "breaking news," so that all of a sudden "safety" comes in the form of a TV news announcer's solution. When we are fearful, we make bad decisions and are often paralyzed and unable to make clear decisions to safeguard ourselves and our families, or to reclaim our self-authority and ability to navigate through the world.

We have been programmed to value safety. There's nothing wrong with safety; it's just that when it comes at the cost of all our freedoms, health and well-being, it's not worth it. Those vying for power over us have—like the man behind the curtain in the Wizard of Oz—manipulated the pandemic to make it look bigger and more fearful than it actually was, in order to lead us willingly into a global inoculation and control program. The strategy is to override and erode our faith in our body's own adaptive and effective immune system responses, in favor of an artificial technological solution to all illnesses with many vaccinations.

We all have an essential role to play in creating a more loving and kind world, and if we are afraid, then we can't fulfill our role and midwife miracles, as is our birthright. We pick up feelings and emotions from each other, they are contagious. Fear latches on very easily in a subtle manner, and we don't notice its arrival unless we pay careful attention to our body and its response to new information.

Fear fractures our protective aura of connection to the Field of Love and thus robs us of the innate power of who we Truly are. What we fear, we energetically connect with, focus upon and thus attract into our experience. Fear undermines our power and lowers our frequency, so finding our way from fear to equanimity is important, so that we aren't immobilized and ensnared by its plan that puts our safety in someone else's hands.

Fear is not a natural state: It is a distortion in our energy field. It is enabled by our misidentification with being our bodies, and our belief that we are separate, disconnected from each other and from the world we live in. When we know we are connected to each other, the Earth and the Field of Love around us, we are less vulnerable to fear and to the stresses of these times. These three inspiring stories illustrate a resiliency to fear that comes from these people knowing who they are.

Peace Pilgrim, Mildred Norman, walked back and forth across the US without any belongings, saying she would "walk until war stopped and there was Peace on Earth." She carried no food, didn't ask for anything, and ate only when it was offered. Once she was invited into a car to get warm. The man planned to rape her.[134] She went to sleep *in complete trust without fear.* Her peaceful sleep and her Love frequency awoke the higher nature and peaceful protector in the man, and he didn't follow through with his plan. Her high frequency Love, which was more coherent, overrode his lower frequency and his actions changed. The banner on her website has this quote: "No one walks as safely as one who walks humbly and harmlessly with great love and great faith."[135]

A woman I will call **Rachel** was in a similarly dangerous situation. She was stripped naked by several men, and it was *Love* that radiated with such energy from her naked body that the men couldn't follow through with their plan, either. There is a higher aspect to us all that helps us through these kinds of dire situations. Call it our Spirit Guides, Guardian Angels, Higher Self, Christ Self, Love incarnate or the Universe. It is our Wild Card, our innate power as our original Creator Self coming through us to influence the world we live in. Sometimes in threatening situations our True Self shines through our physicality and saves the day. Or perhaps it's because in times of great need, we let go of our *resistance* to our True Nature as Love and allow our Eternal everpresent Light to shine through us unimpeded.

---

[134] Peace Pilgrim, Her Life and Work in her own Words, compiled by some of her friends. 1982, Santa Fe New Mexico, Ocean Tree Books. Pg. 31.
[135] https://www.peacepilgrim.org/articles-about-peace-pilgrim

Lama Rangbar Nyimai Ozer,[136] a Tibetan Buddhist, told a story of walking home late at night in Kathmandu in the mountains of Nepal. Stray street dogs mostly sleep through the daytime and then gather together in feral packs at night. One night there was a pack of thirty to forty dogs in the road ahead, and the only way to get home was through the fiercely growling and barking dogs. With Lama's characteristic humor, he shared that "It would be bad policy to run," and he just decided that *whatever they were doing or saying had nothing to do with him, their barking must have something to do with someone else.* As he walked straight through the pack, the dogs stopped barking and quieted. They didn't get any rise of fear out of him. About this he shared, "This is a metaphor for our lives. Everyone is barking their opinions about what we are doing. The phenomenon often barks, too—situations, things, bill collectors, that you could react to. And in that reaction, you explode it; your emotions and chi get involved, and all that happens is that you become exhausted and terrified. The alternative is to stay focused and clear, understand your own intentions and move forward with life. Sometimes accelerating is one way to get out of a situation, as well. A path reveals itself." Lama's story is a template for our path forward. Having moved past our fear, it requires us to keep walking ahead with our focus upon where *we do want to go* and remembering that acceleration may be necessary to get us out of a tight situation!

Peace Pilgrim's, Rachel's and Lama Rangbar Nyimai Ozer's Universal Love protected them. Their Love was so complete they were invulnerable. When our Love is so complete that it can look through our aggressors to a deeper presence within them, *without fear*, our wholeness in those moments is our protection. Our attackers are whole as well and are unable to assault us, seeing their own wholeness in such a clear mirror of Love. In all three stories, their actions were not from fear, they were from the stillness inside themselves which made their confidence,

---

[136] Lama Rangbar Nymai Ozer, a well loved teacher of Tibetan Buddhism, leads a non-profit organization called Bodhivastu, that has centers in the mid-Hudson Valley, and Catskill region of NY state. Bodhivastu.org

clarity, Universal Love and luck possible. Perhaps just one bit of fear would have made these outcomes impossible.

We are Love incarnated in a Field of Love, the purity of the Love that we are helps protect us. It's not something we add to ourselves; it's already there, and we just uncover it within ourselves. Their wholeness made them immune to their fear or gave them strength to overcome their fear.

Fear Inoculation

Dispelling the fear that the global plan engenders is imperative. There is a catch, however: We can't dispel the fear if we don't know what we are afraid of, if we are too afraid to look at it, or if we just don't want to deal with it. So it's important to educate ourselves on this difficult topic. What I understand to be the situation is explained in the Great Reset in a Nutshell, in the Appendix. As a human family, we need to learn what is *actually* going on outside of the mainstream media's carefully choreographed explanation of things, by watching the documentaries and other references listed in the back of the book and reading the World Economic Forum website. The information tears down the safety and security of everything we have relied upon, trusted, and that has supported us. All of our Constitutional Freedoms are now gone. We just have to face it and make a clear choice. Avoiding this knowledge will entrap us. The people behind these plans want to become "masters of the Earth."

I was talking with Ray, who I had just met, about the advantages of facing fearful scenarios in advance of their arrival in order to move beyond the frozen deer-in-the-headlights response to them. He turned out to be an ex-Marine and said, "Yes, of course. We call it *fear inoculation*." By getting used to a fearful scenario, we can find our way past our shock to

> Like a telltale on a sail that shows what direction the wind is blowing, fear can be a useful marker to help us chart our course.

an appropriate response. Fear's resolution brings equanimity and a thoughtful and appropriate response to the fearful scenario.

Fear, when it is not debilitating, can be a messenger. What am I really afraid of? Perhaps it is a call to act in some way. Can I do something about it? What should I do? Do I need to have help? Are there changes I need to make?

A good friend sent me a link to an interview with Aman Jabbi, in 2022, called *The Trojan Horse of the Digital Panopticon,* which laid out the plan to monitor and control humanity, with photos of the infrastructure quietly being built in Jabbi's home state of Montana. Once the infrastructure is in place and operating, with or without our consent, our world becomes an open air prison.[137] The interview was so terrifying, I couldn't watch it through the first time. I didn't want to hear what it was saying, but I realized after a day of discomfort around it that I had to watch the rest. It was like someone was knocking on the front door, and I was trying to ignore it and pretend there was no one out there. So I listened to the entire interview instead of watching it, which was easier for me. My mother, who I was visiting at the time, saw a frozen look on my face afterwards and asked, "Are you ok?" I hadn't been able to speak freely with her, and I took a moment to find my answer and said . . . "No, I am not ok and neither are you, but you just don't know it." It was an opening for a conversation, which was a relief because knowing of these potential future horrors alone is a great burden. At one point she said, "Well, what can any one person do?" feeling the powerlessness that most of us feel at times. I said, "Daddy didn't sit by as the world was being overrun by Hitler. He went to fight. There must be something that we can all do." That is really the question for us all. The process of writing this book has brought me to the answers you will find in these pages. We each have a unique role to play when faced with situations that capture our attention. What answers have you discovered?

---

[137] A term that Amman Jabbi uses in his talk: *The Trojan Horse of the Digital Panopticon. https://www.youtube.com/watch?v=p1i3k-zrYWE*

When the terror subsided after a couple of days, it left me with a background agitation that I just couldn't abide. I realized that in order to find my peace again, I needed to take action. I had noticed surveillance cameras popping up in public places without comment or consent, especially at key intersections and on highways. I decided to create a brochure on the role of surveillance cameras in the Great Reset plan for global control of humanity, that I could share with people to awaken them to this possible scenario. Learning to recognize the wolf in sheep's clothing is a necessary step to successfully asserting our right to our own lives, bodies and to the solutions that will help our world thrive. The brochure reads "What are all those Surveillance Cameras really for? This flyer outlines what is currently being implemented by the United Nations, World Economic Forum, World Health Organization and Global Corporations, their comprehensive plan for 2030 is called: THE GREAT RESET... Are you aware of it?" [138]

It was a huge relief to start writing it, and was relatively easy as Amman Jabbi's interview was a comprehensive outline resource for it. It also pushed me well outside of my comfort zone and made me feel vulnerable. I created the brochure over the next few weeks, which helped me work through the fear I felt. When I returned to visit my mother a few weeks later, I shared the brochure with her. It made her uncomfortable, but she read it, and later even suggested I share it with someone at a gathering we were at. When I went into almost all the stores in her small town to share the brochure, I found many people open to reading it, and a few

---

[138] The brochure is available for download at https://www.freedomsart.com/offerings

who were already aware of the Great Reset. The process was healing at every stage. And in passing the flyers out, I realized I wasn't the only one alarmed at the situation and concerned about the future. Talking about it helps.

> Our comfort zone is like a garden encircled by a white picket fence. It is time to move out of it, past our fears and into the world, to get to work creating, building and speaking about our New Earth built from Love.

Moving beyond our fear is an evolutionary and transformational process initiated from our inner self that knows no fear. I have systematically observed things that made me fearful, and have moved to dissolve the fear I felt, by facing them head on. This process of moving through our fears, makes more space for our courage, and for our full identity since we are actually beings both in this world and outside of this world. In fear, we distort our connection to our expansive True Self, which by its nature is whole, loving and secure. Fear creates tension and energy blockages that we can feel in our bodies, and blocks the clarity of our thought. If we notice where fear inhabits our body we can just watch it, be present with it. As we accept fear's presence as simply "what is" in the moment, it can loosen because we aren't rejecting it. This takes the sting of fear out of us. There's no need to craft big stories around fear, just let it pass through. I stop wherever I am and become absolutely still. It's like hitting a reset button. I may have to stop again in ten minutes, but it really helps the fear to dissipate. Change is a constant here on Earth, and change is happening faster and faster even in the processing of fear. As the frequency rises on Earth, there is more Light, so fear and powerlessness—like the dust-bunnies in the back of our closets—can now be seen and swept away more easily.

What can we do when faced with such fear inducing scenarios? We can know that we are powerful. We are created of the creator. We are whole. We, like all beings, hold the pinnacle of Human Light Existence. It is not logical to be fearful if we are like a lion in the jungle. Know this: say, "I am like a lion in the jungle." Attune to the Love and the frequency of interconnectedness all around us. Standing in the role of a creator being. There is a responsibility we have as well: to create in the direction that we want to move. We can imagine a beautiful world. We can also know that the forces that are hard at work otherwise have no basis in Truth.

What is your response to fearful news or situations? Our strategy can be to walk ahead as though there were no trap. As though there were only Love we can live our life. As though the land beneath our feet were sacred and secure, we can walk forward. There is nothing that can harm us as this is done. It is evidenced by the stories I have shared of Peace Pilgrim and Lama Rangbar. Who and how we are inside determines what happens around us.

It is, however, prudent to be aware of the mainstream world, for the agenda of control does exist, and it does have the potential to hurt us. We must be careful, wise and paying attention to our inner guidance as we walk ahead.

Our words of Love and affection for the Earth and for our fellow humans are potent, and such potency is what heals the rift between all of us and the Earth. In beginning a strategy of this sort, the first steps are the hardest. Once you see that our world is secure then you are more confident moving forward. It is healing and Light[139] that will form the energy bridge from this world to the next one, where such evil does not exist. And so, in multidimensional thought we must think, in awareness that all is of a Higher Order we are saved. This heightened sense of

---

[139] I thought I would ask my higher self : What do you mean by Light? I received: *"Light as I have used it here means the emanation, the spark that shines from a love-filled, joyful, happy, content human. One who is organized to attend to the whole affair of shifting the Earth up a notch or two. As you are in harmony with your environment something occurs that adds Light to the body. Light can be a transmission of energy to another by just a glance; you meet their eye and the spark in your eye lights theirs—and exchange occurs wordlessly, although a smile accelerates this possibility. Thank You."*

identity as Consciousness and Love is ours to hold and share and be. It simply needs to be asked for, aligned with, demonstrated. Our capacity to demonstrate this is for ourself as much as for anyone who benefits. (We must save ourselves before we can save anyone else.) And so be sure that all is well, that the good guys win, that there is no superior thought; there is only Love that will carry us through all this and create a peaceful world.

> In the same way that the hefty lady chef, cooking for my sister's wedding stepped out of her underwear when it dropped around her ankles, we must step out of fear, or fear will trip us up.

We can walk with awareness of the hazards, knowing we are secure, as we stand up for our rights. There is a saying that seems relevant: "Fake it till you make it." Fake your invulnerability, confidence and security until you notice it is actually present. Our Loving energy is more coherent than that of fear, coercion and separation. Not consenting to the encroaching regulations around the Great Reset may bring up a sense of fear and vulnerability as we make these difficult and important choices. Just keep walking forward on your path until you feel the confidence of the choice you are making. We have the wind of the Universe at our backs.

This quote from *Becoming*, about our safety, is reassuring:

> *Since all that exists as manifest reality is vibrational, those that exist in a vibratory rate that is harmonious with the planet will find themselves in safe places. Those safe places will exist where these individuals are. There are no "safe places" as designated on the planet despite any and all predictions. There will be safe places in the midst of any and all disaster experiences. It is the consciousness of the individuals themselves that will create those places.*[140]

---

[140] *Becoming*, Hayden ID, Bridger House Publishers, INC., pg.100.

Courage

We associate courage with an act when it is guarded by fear. Courage is a word that is linked with *coeur*, the French word for "heart." An inspiring cause empowers heart-full courageous action. Living within our passion and Truth gives us the strength to be courageous. Our compliance is needed to make this Global Reset plan work, so speaking out and the courage of non-compliance is essential to change the future we are heading towards. Non-compliance gets easier the more we do it. Our courage grows the more we exercise it. (No more fatty couch potato courage!)

> Your higher self has an expanded perspective and communicates to you through your somatic feelings and instincts and through joyful, challenging and loving ideas.

Discovering the global plan for world control is like waking up in a bad dream. I sometimes call it a grade B horror movie, complete with villains, victims and heroes. Learning of the global plan brings up fear, disbelief, incredulity and anger. Not knowing about this plan does not protect us; *"Passive agreement through ignorance is still agreement."* [141] In our unawareness of this plan, and our not resisting this plan, we are agreeing with this plan. Our consent is implicit when we say and do nothing that opposes the plan's enactment.

---

[141] *Becoming*, Author not named, Idaho, Bridger House Publishers Inc. pg 183.

CH VI RETRACT OUR CONSENT

Private, closely held control of ALL central banks, and hence of all money creation, has allowed a very few people to control all political parties and governments; the intelligence agencies and their myriad front organizations; the armed forces and the police; the major corporations and, of course, the media. These very few people are the prime movers. Their plans are executed over decades. Their control is opaque. To be clear, it is these very few people, who are hidden from you, who are behind this scheme to confiscate all assets, who are waging a hybrid war against humanity. — David Rogers Webb, *The Great Taking*

Who are These Brazen Globalists?

This answer to that important question is from the *Handbook for The New Paradigm*:

> *Who indeed has set this up and is pulling the strings. Is it really just a group of somebodies that is in charge? . . . The Truth is that there are multiple levels of activity behind what appears to be a play of incredible magnitude. Who then is writing the lines for the characters and what is the point of the script? Would it be a surprise to inform you that you are writing the lines and until you can figure out*

a point to the script, there is none? If that is the case, then which of the individuals on the planet can figure one out? Well, indeed there is a focused group that has decided that they would like to put forth their point in the script. There is just one problem with this, they have decided to put forth a focus within the play that is not in harmony with the Creator of the stage, and the theatre that this play is to be performed upon. In fact, the plan this group has in mind has a great surprise at the end for the audience and the actors on the stage. They intend to destroy the audience, the actors, the stage and the theatre.

> I sometimes use the 'deathbed' test to gauge my actions… would I regret *doing* or *not doing* something in a life review at the end of my time on Earth?

Since the Creator of this theatre likes this particular theatre and thinks of it as a pet project, this idea doesn't appeal to Him at all.[142]

Warnings such as this simply cannot be and shouldn't be ignored, especially not when there is so much clear evidence to support them. When we ignore this, we ignore it at our own peril, and selfishly toss our children and grandchildren and perhaps many more generations into a very harsh life, perhaps bereft of the things that make life worth living.

In addition, there is evidently one all-controlling person at the top of the financial pyramid that, like a puppeteer, wields the strings that make the heads of governments, corporations and Non-Governmental Organizations (NGO's) dance to their music. Their will determines what happens.[143] And, in fact they own almost everything on Earth. *The Great Taking*, by David Rogers Webb, follows the trail of power and

---

[142] *Handbook fro the New Paradigm*, pg 1-2. The Creator mentioned is the Creator "God" of this Earth.

[143] Vladimir Megre, *The New Civilization*, The Ringing Cedars of Russia Series.

control to the evidence that "the protected class" can claim ownership of all things, without the true owners having any recourse. In addition, the structure of capitalism can be seen as a pyramid, where directives from the top trickle down and control the actions of governments, corporations, non-profits and all parts of the world entrained with money. It is not only done through money, but through the use of the Laws of Nature—The Laws of Creation.[144]

Carefully set for many generations, the multilayer control plan is woven together with off-planet beings, hybridized humans, shadow controllers—and humans who have sided with these beings, voluntarily or unknowingly, and also through coercion, blackmail, bribery and addiction. **Proving all this is not my intention here. Others have already done this.**[145] Piecing together the scene we face in the theater of Earth we are all in has been done by many truth-seeking humans. They are modern day super-heroes who are willing to speak the truth they discovered, to awaken and secure freedom for the entire human family, at great risk to themselves. I simply share the plan as it appears right now, as a rather dire and tangled trap that can be seen from many levels and perspectives. **Please do all humanity your children and yourself a favor and investigate this for yourself.** Go online to Rumble, Patreon, BitChute and other servers that have not curtailed free speech as completely as mainstream news sources and social media have. The "fact checkers"[146] that many innocently see as the "arbiters of truth" are not. They are just one layer in a multi-layer control plan to keep us ignorant of where we are going as a human family and what

---

[144] Quoting a story that Anastasia told; Megre, Vladimir, in *The New Civilization*, 2005, Ringing Cedars Press, HI, pg 81.
[145] David Martin's dossier, https://archive.org/details/the-fauci-covid-19-dossier_202109; *Plandemic, Plandemic 2*, and Plandemic 3, https etc. awakening-movie; *Thrive, Thrive 2*, https etc.WQX50; Del Bigtree https etc. bigtree/; Elana Freeland, an interview with Elana Freeland author of *Geoengineered Transhumanism: How the Environment Has Been Weaponized By Chemicals, Electromagnetics, and Nanotechnology For Synthetic Biology*, https://rumble.com/v24rim4-geoengineered-transhumanism-elana-freeland-and-ana-mihalcea-md-phd.htm, and many more.
[146] https://www.acsh.org/news/2019/11/04/debunkers-debunked-who-fact-checks-fact-checkers-14378, one of several similar articles.

will happen when we get there. If you see the words "disinformation" or "misinformation," dig deeper. In the documentary *Never Again Is Now Global*,[147] it described that when Jewish people were being gathered up to board the trains for concentration camps, they were told a different story to entice them to come willingly. We are all being lured in the same manner to a very negative future.

Chaos And False Flags

One of the methods of moving a whole society towards a specific mindset is to create false flag events and chaos. A false flag event (a mass shooting, a war, an accident, a crash, a disaster) and the media's urgent information about it, distracts us from what is being enacted quietly somewhere behind the scenes and out of sight. False flag[148] events [definition in footnote] are being created and inflated to keep us focused upon them, when we ought to remain focused upon *what is happening behind the scenes or afterwards*, as the result of these attention grabbing events. The manufactured, or optimized natural situations, are designed to create chaos, fear and instability to the degree that the people then ask for solutions that instill further control, with more limitations, like gun control, in order to keep us safe. The Patriot Act[149] is a classic example of this technique, which was maneuvered in rapidly after 9/11/01, though it had been written well in advance, waiting for the right time and circumstances to be pushed through without due deliberation. This methodology is clever, diabolical and manipulates with great skill. It is one way of herding the populace into greater limitations on all our Constitutionally protected freedoms. Learning to recognize a false flag

---

[147] From the documentary *Never Again Is Now Global*. https://www.avclub.com/film/reviews/never-again-is-now-global-2023

[148] A **false flag** operation is an act committed with the intent of disguising the actual source of responsibility and pinning blame on another party. The term "false flag" originated in the 16th century as an expression meaning an intentional misrepresentation of someone's allegiance. Wikipedia.

[149] The Patriot Act was passed 5 weeks after the 9/11 bombings, and allows the government to use surveillance on its own citizens, in the war on domestic terrorism. It was renewed in 2015.

helps us to be less subject to its manipulation. False flag events require level-headed and measured responses. As this multilayer global control plan runs its course, *chaos* is a likely stage we will go through. We can't let chaos unbalance us. We can stay grounded, calm and alert, and realize that chaos may be a necessary part of the revealing and the healing process of transitioning to a New Earth Paradigm.

> Writing about these topics of Global control is not easy. It stirs up a lot of turbulent emotions. The winter sun illuminates the frost lining all the bare twigs and branches, and right now all is calm and fine. I awoke from a dream this morning where a large number of us spent a night in an empty new house. In the dream as we were cleaning up the next morning, I tried to scrub away a staring face looking down out of the sky. The face then moved to be on the floor and then it was in the toilet bowl. Its power and threat disappeared when it was seen below me.

I think this could be how it is with the global plan, a huge mirage of power that, in the end, simply doesn't exist for us as Consciousness in the Field of Love, as Lions in the Jungle and as men and women[150] created by a Loving Creator. Everything we thought was so fearful is small in comparison to who we are. The knowledge of who we are and where our power comes from is what Globalists don't want us to remember. It is because we are so powerful that we are being targeted in this way, so that our power becomes and remains, our aggressors' power.

Our Purpose Here On Earth

A key weakness of our human families, as was mentioned in the above quote from *Handbook for the New Paradigm* is that we have forgotten or lost sight of our purpose on this Earth and have fallen asleep. We

---

[150] *The Law for Mankind Knowledge Share* explains the power of our birth as men and women.

have forgotten who we are and what a sacred opportunity this physical body brings to us, *to live in apparent separation and love as though we are connected!*

This global control situation can be seen as a gift, or an alarm call. It can awaken us, hopefully in time, to do what we need to do to set things right, to adjust our course and create a new path forward. It's as simple as recalibrating our systems of life to Love. We are all One Consciousness appearing in many forms, and I believe **our purpose is to Love and uplift each other and create a beautiful life upon the Earth. When we remember and incorporate our True Self beyond-the-body into the here and now, we have access to the unconditional love of our greater self.** We exist in many dimensions. We evolve, transform and become more wise over time as we are able to translate our experiences into wisdom,[151] and we can then navigate the Earth with greater skill, compassion and love. By moving out of fear and separation from all that surrounds us into Love and self responsibility we can access more of our multidimensional selves and create a new kind of world.

Gabor Lukacs lived in Rumania at a time that in order to survive you had to be in community, to trade for food, clothing and other needs. He observed how in America, with our democracy and affluence, we don't need each other in this same way. Instead we just need money. Money has superseded the role that community played in the past. In our culture it is considered a badge of honor that we don't have to ask for help from anyone. Our communities are designed so that we are all separate, often not even knowing our neighbors, as we drive into our garages without setting foot outside our home. It's also rare to work together with another family or to trade anything. Perhaps this transition will give us the opportunity and desire to get to know our neighbors at another level of mutual support, loving interaction and intentional community-building.

---

[151] *Handbook for the New Paradigm, Embracing the Rainbow, Becoming...* it is mentioned throughout the trilogy of books.

Not knowing what to do in the face of this information is no reason not to do something. Talk with your family, friends, neighbors, and local sheriff and police about it, we gain strength when we join together. Ask your conscience, your heart, your intuition, your Higher Self or ask the Universe, "What shall I do?" If your answer is loving, do it. **Trust that you are powerful, capable and perfectly created to fulfill your role**. Sometimes sitting very, very still is the most powerful "doing." And sometimes our "doing" requires shouting from the roof tops!

I was guided to mention the Founding Fathers of the United States of America in this book. They faced threats not unlike what we face now. I am not calling for violence or to dump tea but, instead, for us to deeply reflect upon their extraordinary courage to stand up for their own freedoms. We, too, have this critical role to take on as we move through these challenging times and stand up for our rights. They boycotted tea at the start of the American Revolution. We can peacefully and lovingly take our money and business away from the companies associated with supporting this Global control plan, in order to create a very different future. Surprisingly, our grounding in the Field of Love is one of the keys. Love is the ultimate power. So start from Love for yourself, your children and for the Earth—*not from attack*—in removing yourself from the systems of control. This holds your frequency high, and keeps you operating at a higher level than the negative control program functions at. It's time for a revolution of Love, by peaceful means.

America has a leadership role on Earth. This image is of Liberty Climbing the Ladder of Consciousness with the Earth on her back, illustrates our task now, to carry the world to safety by raising our Consciousness.

Money, Banks and Investments

It seems logical to extricate ourselves from the old world's systems that are supporting the global plan, and doing harm. Your money, how you spend it, where you invest it, and what you create more of by using it, matters. The money supply in the US is regulated and created by the

Federal Reserve Bank,[152] which is not part of the US government. It is its own separate entity. The Federal Reserve controls the money supply and by proxy the economy and the government. It is in service to its owners, not the people of the US. This quote from *The Great Taking* explains: "The Fed chairman does not work for the public; he works for the people who own and control the Fed. You are not allowed to know who these people are."[153]

This quote from John Root explains the power of banking:

> *The powers that be promote the problem as "human nature," in other words inevitable. The problem is not human nature. The problem is that whoever is issuing the currency is the sovereign. Money is always issued by the law giver, as a matter of law. We will only be sovereign when we are issuing the currency. What the currency is issued for orients the activity of the people. The currencies of the world are all issued by banks as interest-bearing debt to themselves. Therefore society is all about paying tribute to the hidden sovereign in the form of interest on money the banks create when we promise to make it valuable [with our labor]. All the money is issued for what will be profitable for banks. The banking cartel has such a huge percentage of the wealth that they succeed in keeping us debt and wage slaves. It is up to those of us who recognize the technocratic transhumanist totalitarian tiptoe to affirm to each other our true nature and create Heaven on Earth!*"[154]

Now there is a phrase: ". . . the technocratic transhumanist totalitarian tiptoe . . ."! Those are the global controllers who have tiptoed into our

---

[152] https://www.federalreserve.gov/aboutthefed/the-fed-explained.htm
[153] David Rogers Webb, 2023, *The Great Taking* pg xxix, David Rogers Webb.
[154] John G Root, https://www.justabundance.org/ John Root's book, *Freedom, Justice and Community,* (not yet published) outlines how we can create self-governing communities that issue money to support the priorities of the people without interest or debt.

world and our lives and are imposing their future vision on us with our time, money, life force and energy. We are not helpless, just asleep to what is happening and to what we need to do and create in order to stop it.

If you think John's words on bankers were a bit strong, here is an even more condemning quote on banking from a banker himself:

> *The modern banking system manufactures money out of nothing. The process is perhaps the most astounding piece of sleight of hand that was ever invented. Banking was conceived in inequity and born in sin. Bankers own the Earth. Take it away from them but leave them the power to create money, and with a flick of a pen, they will create enough money to buy it back again. Take this great power away from them and all great fortunes like mine will disappear, for then this would be a better and happier world to live in. But if you want to continue to be the slaves of bankers and pay the cost of your own slavery, then let bankers continue to create money and control credit.* — Sir Josiah Stamp, President of the Rothschild Bank of England and the 2nd richest man in Britain in the 1920's speaking at the University of Texas in 1927.

In the interest of transparency, my father and grandfather were bankers. My former husband was an investment banker. I consider them honest and loving people. A New Earth paradigm will perhaps bring a very different role for money, banking and exchange. Several books have been written on the future of money, exchange and gifting economics and are listed in the bibliography.

What Future Are We Investing In?

In addition, our investments may be playing a role in supporting this negative global plan. BlackRock, Vanguard, State Street and other monolithic investment corporations bundle groups of stocks into vast investment funds. The investment funds that these types of huge companies offer, may hold the stocks of other companies that may destroy, harm and undermine human health and freedoms, pillage, plunder and break up the perfect systems of Nature, and strip the living and diverse resources of the Earth. All without the investor having any knowledge of it. Dangerous, untested and destructive technologies are making many humans rich at enormous expense to the Earth and the health of all humanity. There are many more millionaires now than there were in 2019 when all this began. This is part of the plan.

> I had to laugh at this line from *The Great Taking*: "If you are wealthy and think you are special, you are special. They are saving you for dessert."[155]

The buildout of 5G is a prime example. Its infrastructure continued to be built out during the pandemic, making money for stockholders, when so many other businesses were forced to close their doors. It is time to choose investments that promote and support a positive future. Using our money wisely, carefully and with discernment is part of our power and our responsibility. Social, environmental and non-violent parameters can all be used in evaluating whether a stock or a fund is a suitable non-harming investment. The World Economic Forum's Environment Social Governance (ESG) program designation is part of the control plan.

> *"To escape from this agenda, you must unlearn all that holds you captive to it."* -Amman Jabbi

Reduce Our Online Data

Recalling the quote from Chapter IV, "If you have enough data and enough computing power then you can understand people better than they understand themselves, and then you can manipulate them in ways that were previously impossible." It takes work to reduce our online data exposure, but knowing of this plan, and how heartless and

---

[155] *The Great Taking*, Page 66.

aggressive the plan is—to remove our free will and to separate us from our souls—gives us the motivation to change our ways. Will we sell our souls for convenience? Or make the choices necessary to reduce our exposure to the control program at this level. It may mean getting rid of our cell phones. Isn't that name, "cell phone," ironic? It puts us in a jail cell of 24/7 surveillance and, like some of this control agenda, is hidden in plain sight. There are many things that we can do to limit online interactions. We can join a group like the Privacy Action Plan[156] for guidance on how to prevent our data and information from being captured by the internet, and data bases where it is sold.

Use Cash

"Keep Cash Alive" is a successful campaign that brought to the world's attention the importance of using cash in daily transactions. Without cash all transactions are tracked and monitored, and a percentage is taken by the system that does the electronic transaction. I try to pay with cash, and when I do I give out a slip of a paper that says

> **I paid cash today for a reason :-)**
>
> 1. To SAVE this business money on transaction fees
> 2. To GIVE this business more control over their profits
> 3. To SUPPORT my local economy and community
> 4. To KEEP my purchases and location anonymous
> 5. To KEEP cash alive!
>
> Using cash can be inconvenient...but what if it's worth it? Here's a 2-minute read, see what you think...
> www.keepcashalive.com

Shopkeepers are often deeply touched by this message. I return to stores months later and see the paper I gave them taped to the check out counter.

---

[156] The Privacy Action Plan, an online resource listed in the Rays of Hope and reasons to prevail section. https://privacyactionplan.com/

Say No To Cameras. Cover the cameras on your phone (both front and back cameras), computer, TV and other devices. Say no to the cameras behind every checkout and at important intersections by saying with respect and gentleness "I do not consent to my image being taken and used or sold by you, because there is a plan to control us all via their use." I was told by someone who's friend is in the surveillance camera business that even the private cameras can be easily hacked into when they are connected to wifi.

> Buy and use faraday bags for your phone, computer and other WIFI-connected devices for location and data privacy and an environment free of Electro Magnetic Frequencies.

Grow your own food, even if it is window box on your balcony or windowsill. Stockpile some food and water, and things you might need for a disaster. Join a CSA, a Community Share Exchange, for fresh vegetables in season, frequent farmers markets, connect with your local farmers and buy direct. The list, "Rays of Hope," in the back of the book offers some other resources for self sufficiency, and many groups and individuals doing amazing work in creation of the New Earth. What would you do if the grocery store wasn't there?

> Having a larger cause and meaning for our life gives us the courage, power and energy to persevere through challenging times.

Work towards Self Responsibility. Exit the consumer lifestyle. Examine your practices in relationship with the Earth, resources and energy. Simplify. Reuse, reduce, re-purpose, recycle, respect the creatures—liberate the spiders from your home, don't kill them; compassionate acts little and big are important. Share large machinery and tools with your neighbors and friends. Fix and repair, build conservatively with Nature in mind.

Work to make free energy devices available. Compost. Teach vegetable gardening to one person each year. Start a community clothing swap. Frequent thrift stores. Live more lightly upon the Earth. Thank her often. Spread Love.

Non-Compliance and Satyagraha

Mahatma Gandhi's *Satyagraha*, or "truth force," defined by Gandhi's biographer, Louis Fischer, as "to be strong not with the strength of the brute but with the strength of the spark of God." It's a natural way of being that has been trained out of us by our default referencing of the outer world in all things. In approaching this task of extricating ourselves from the grasp of the old world's structures, it is worth calling upon our satyagraha, the force of our Truth. . . our inner sourced Truth, as we move to reapportion our resources, money and the people we trust with our money and our business in the world.

The corporations of this world are fatally flawed for serving as our leaders on Earth because they are in service to their shareholders, not the public, the environment or the greater good of all life. Gerry Mander said it succinctly: "U.S. corporate law holds that management of publicly held companies must act primarily in the economic interest of shareholders. If not, management can be sued by shareholders and firings would surely occur."[157]

The World Economic Forum has 100 partners, member Corporations. The website says, "The partners believe in the power of collaboration to drive positive change, and work closely with the World Economic Forum to help shape industry, regional and global agendas"[158] Here they are listed:

---

[157] *In the Absence of The Sacred, The Failure of Technology & the Survival of the Indian Nations*, by Jerry Mander, pg 123
[158] WEF Website https://www.weforum.org/communities/strategic-partnership-b5337725-fac7-4f8a-9a4f-c89072b96a0d

ABB Accenture, Adani Group, Adecco Group, African Rainbow Minerals, Agility, **AIG**, Aker, Alibaba Group, AlixPartners, Allianz, **Amazon**, Aramco, ArcelorMittal, **AstraZeneca**, Bahrain Economic Development, **Board Bain & Company**, Bajaj Group, Banco Bradesco, Banco Santander, **Bank of America, Barclays, Bill & Melinda Gates Foundation**, BlackRock, **Boston Consulting Group (BCG), BP,** Bridgewater Associates, Hubert Burda Media Capgemini, **Chevron, Cisco, Citi, The Coca-Cola Company,** Cognizant, **Dell Technologies, Deloitte,** Dentsu, **Deutsche Bank, DHL Group,** DP World, dsm-firmenich, EY, **Goldman Sachs, Google,** Hanwha Group, HCLTech, **Hewlett Packard Enterprise, Hitachi, Honeywell,** Hong Kong Exchanges and Clearing (HKEX), HP, HSBC, Huawei Technologies, **IBM**, Infosys, Intel, Itaú, Unibanco, JLL, **Johnson & Johnson, JPMorgan Chase & Co.**, Kearney, KPMG, Kudelski Group, **Lazard,** Luksic Group, Mahindra Group, Majid Al Futtaim Holding, ManpowerGroup, **Marsh McLennan, Mastercard, McKinsey & Company,** Mercuria Energy Group, Meta, **Microsoft, Mitsubishi Corporation, Mitsubishi Heavy Industries, Morgan Stanley,** Mubadala Investment, MUFG Bank, **Nestlé**, Novartis, Novo Nordisk Foundation, Open Society Foundations, Palantir Technologies, **PayPal, PepsiCo, Pfizer,** PwC, **Procter & Gamble,** Publicis Groupe, Qatar Investment Authority, Qualcomm, Reliance Industries, **Royal Philips,** Salesforce, SAP, Saudi Basic Industries (SABIC), Schneider Electric, Sequoia Capital, **Siemens,** SOCAR (State Oil Company of the Azerbaijan Republic), **Sony Group,** S&P Global Standard Chartered Bank, Suntory Holdings, **Swiss Re**, Takeda Pharmaceutical, Tata Consultancy Services, Ericsson, Trafigura, **Uber Technologies, UBS, Unilever, Verizon Communications, Visa, Volkswagen Group Volvo Group,** Wellcome Trust, Wipro, Yara International, Zurich Insurance Group.

In addition, **Anser** (is in charge of Operation Warp Speed), **Fors Marsh Group** (is in charge of Vaccine Marketing), **Palantir** (is in charge of Gotham Data Tracking) and **Publicis sapiens** (Health and Human Services {HHS} Information Technology) were pointed out by David

Martin as the companies that made all the money during the Covid Plan. He calls them "The Privateers."[159]

These corporations, and others who are not listed here who have aligned with the World Economic Forum (WEF), through the Environment Social Governance (ESG)[160] program are supporting the global control agenda of The Great Reset and the radical changes scheduled for 2030.[161] In saying "I do not consent" and disengaging from those systems, our actions align with our beliefs, desires and passions and we raise our frequency as we become more congruent. The advisor to this WEF Group is the one who said "free will is over." The leader of the WEF said "who masters those technologies will be master of the world."[162]

Like a cancer throughout a body, the Control plan has infiltrated the entire surface of the Earth. It has bribed and hypnotized humanity with money and convenience. We have relied on these numerous companies for our many daily wants and needs. Extricating ourselves from their grasp is a very important and difficult choice to make. This is a lifestyle change and takes some significant effort. It won't happen overnight, but taking steady action towards it will help us create a different kind of world and send a message that needs to be heard. There are crimes that have been committed against humanity, and these organizations and companies have participated and gained from what has harmed and killed many of our friends, family and co-workers.[163]

---

[159] David Martin's speech to the Weston A Price Foundation,(at the end of his talk). https://www.bitchute.com/video/fHhniBm4cyiM/
[160] Environmental, Social Governance, ESG is a program to rate, regulate and fine companies; organizations must comply.
[161] Link to the WEF listing of partners: https://www.weforum.org/partners#search; It is rather interesting that three of the major Covid19 vaccine makers are among the partners, perhaps a significant conflict of interest.
[162] https://plandemicseries.com/watch-the-great-awakening-movie/ at the 23 minute mark, spoke by former Chairman of the WEF Klaus Schwab.
[163] David Martin's speech to the Weston A Price Foundation, https://www.bitchute.com/video/fHhniBm4cyiM/

Handbook for the New Paradigm says this change of direction requires a full 180 degree turn:

> *It is necessary to understand that any other degree of turn, short of an 180 degree turn in the opposite direction, will not work! Those that have made the decision to commit to the birthing of a new paradigm must make it their primary focus. What the opposing faction is focusing upon must be held in the peripheral vision. When their plans and actions are faced fully and embraced with fear it gives them the desired energetic support and aids them greatly in accomplishing their goals. It is important to be aware of their plan but to remain focused on the new paradigm that fits like a hand into the glove of creation.*
>
> *The glove is simply awaiting mankind to place their hand within it.*
>
> — Embracing the Rainbow, pgs.123- 124.

The decision becomes less burdensome when we understand the many reasons why making these changes is important, not just for our own lives, freedom and sovereignty, but for all the next seven generations. The global infrastructure (of satellites, surveillance cameras, Artificial Intelligence, central bank digital currencies, a cashless society, digital IDs, vaccine passports, LED street lights with drone charging stations, 5G covering the Earth, Smart Cities, and internment camps) creates an open air prison that our children's children will be captured within, if we allow it to be built out *and put into action*.

A different and positive way of life is possible, and as more of us choose it, the easier it becomes for us all to create or find it. We can create new economies of sharing and gifting to fulfill these same niches, and support new and existing companies that we can be proud to give our business to. What if a perfect circle gifting economy were created? What if we could source locally and regionally everything we need? What if WE issued the money, and all the value we created by its use was returned to us and our communities?[164]

> *"I believe that for every spot of darkness, there is a corresponding point of glory."*[165]

— VictoryBoyd

Let's set the children up for freedom from this system. Let us be the instigators of the glory that our world will experience in the next decades. Lives of deep satisfaction and joy are possible.

---

[164] John Root,
[165] https://plandemicseries.com/victory-boyd-national-anthem/

CH VII SINGULAR FOCUS

The Universe is a participatory system that evolves as a whole, through the choices we make individually and collectively. Empower conscious choice-making and participation.

— *EARTHwise Constitution for a Planetary Civilization*, 6.5[166]

As we are working to extricate ourselves from the Old World's Systems, our thoughts influence material form.[167] Thoughts have substance. What we think matters. "Thoughts become things."[168] Our deliberate intent to create a New Earth Paradigm based in Love comes from our spontaneous inspired words, actions, prayers, declarations, songs, poems, meetings, yearnings, work days, meditations, sharing, gifting, ceremonies, sacred exchange and thoughts. Our intent can help us to fly high above the third dimension and density, to alight on a lighter, higher frequency Earth. New things are possible, as the frequency of the Earth has risen. Watered by joy, warmed by Light, our thoughts will help seed, sprout and grow a Love-filled New Earth of freedom and human sovereignty.

Where our thoughts go, energy flows—*Nicole Matoushek*[169]

---

[166] https://www.earthwisecentre.org/constitution, section 6.5
[167] March Newkirk, *The Astounding Convergence of Physics and Metaphysics, Part I.*
[168] Mike Dooley, *Choose Them Wisely: Thoughts Become Things!* https://www.audiobooks.com/audiobook/54929/?refId=38981&refId=40912&msclkid=e368cbf9251312674e08ae5ce27af18d
[169] Matoushek, Nicole, *What I forgot the day I was born.*

Supported by our actions, Nature's Laws and with our Source Creator on our side nothing can stop this transformation from happening. Visionaries have a role to play in this transition. Artists, singers, song writers, dreamers, inventors, teachers, designers and poets inspire us to know what to create. They help us to imagine, see, hear and feel what is possible. There are visionary powerhouses that are helping the future to take form, perhaps you are one of them. My friend Deborah is one.

Deborah's Visions of the Future

Deborah Roberts has been seeing images of the future for many years. Unable to share them with her family and friends, who belittled her visions, she has held them in sacred silence for much of her life. Realizing that their beauty and insight might inspire others if they knew what was possible for our world, she shared them with me in 2023.

Deborah's life was at a crisis point in 1975. She was alone in a hotel room, reading a Gideon Bible, reviewing some of the scriptures she had memorized as a child (born to evangelical Christian missionaries in Brazil). "I was sitting there at the desk and the next thing I knew, I was not in my body anymore. I was up in the actual firmament. It was a dark October night, clear with a silver moon. I could see all the stars. Up in that space, I was shown very quickly, the answers to every single question one could possibly have about the meaning of life—the answers infused my whole being. Then, I was shown a panorama of thousands of my own personal past lives. I was that, and then I was that, and then I was that. Very fast, at the speed of thought: click click click click click. Each was enough for recognition and very experience-able. Then everything slowed down and I was brought back into the room by a man, I've thought to this day was Jesus. I believed and experienced it then. I felt that recognition.

He said: ***"Every single person on the planet has to experience the Truth of I AM."***[170]

Deborah continued: "I was brought up to believe I was a sinner from hell. Hearing this [higher truth] from Jesus was very foreign to me: that we all have to come to terms with the I AM-ness of each of us. And then I was brought back into the hotel room. My body was sitting there where I had left it. My head was leaning over, slumped heavily on the desk. I looked pretty dead. The lamp light was yellowish and dull, compared to the bright and beautiful Light of the Christ that I saw. So this Being of Light gently put me back in my body and I lifted my head up and opened my eyes. I was a new person."

> Focus on where you want to go, hold the frequency and emotion you would have if you were *already there*.

"The Truth of I AM" is that we must know ourselves as One Consciousness and live from that knowledge. This is a key to our positive future.

> The world is as we dream it! May we choose our dreams wisely! -Margaret Arndt, Secretary of Just Abundance, Inc.

At another time, while lying in bed, Deborah saw a vision of the Earth hovering above her. It was so real, it was like she could reach out and touch it. As she watched, the Earth separated into two. One Earth drifted up to the left, and the original Earth drifted down to the right. As she watched them fully separate, it was evident that there was greater light coming from the one floating upward. Then she heard a voice that said **"Where you put**

---

[170] I believe this means that everyone must remember and experience who we are as non-dual Consciousness, or the eternal Source and spark of infinity.

your attention is where you will be. Keep your attention on the one going up and you will be with the one going up, the other one is just phasing out, if you have your attention on that, then you will just phase out with that one." Deborah never watched TV or any other media, and she became curious to know what was happening on the Earth that was dropping down and phasing out. Her media-binge discovery of "many terrible things like child trafficking, satanic ritual abuse, programming of people, lies about everything, including the Covid vaccine, and the pandemic" helped to cement her resolve: "I'm going to focus on the Light one."

I so appreciate the message in Deborah's vision, that **we don't need to fight the dark forces on the Earth to hasten their demise. They are simply going to phase out as we render their world obsolete** by the creation of, and participation with, a higher frequency Earth, one that we do want to live upon. The athletic team mantra "the best defense is a good offense" comes to mind. Our good offense is each of us actively envisioning, creating, dreaming, expressing and keeping our focus, words and actions locked upon a New Earth. We don't need to put our energy into defending ourselves when we have so many exciting and positive things to create. Building the New Earth into full physical expression is going to be done through millions of individuals understanding the Laws of Creation and using them proactively. We can see it in our mind's eye, believe it is possible and simply start heading towards it. Others will join us as we go along.

Your Role

These times require bold, fearless and open hearted action towards creating a more evolved world (as the old one dismantles). When we create a future that is beautiful, nurturing, exciting and inspiring, our contrasting grievances, wounds, victimhood and even our sorrows, become less interesting and diminish in their power to capture our focus and emotional energy. In this higher frequency world we can move past all that has blocked us from this evolutionary change in the past. We have much support for this change, as our higher selves increasingly become present here on this higher frequency Earth. Our *clear sight, willingness* and *follow-through* catalyze the Universe's supportive engagement with us, and this is where the fun begins! We each have a role to play in these times and so what we end up doing will be somewhat natural for us. We have been training for this all our lives! Perhaps we will take what we have done in the past to the next level.

> *The role that is yours to fulfill must become evident to you, and it must be a role that is natural and yet too, a bit daunting, for if it is not a bit daunting, then you are not thinking BIG enough. And so delight in this! Gather with your friends and families to discuss this need, and the naturally organizing systems of food, water, shelter, communication, energy and light—internal and external—so that we might move ahead with a shared focus and so the needs will be fulfilled.*
>
> *As this is occurring in the outer world there are forces that would oppose such union among men and women (and those who don't call themselves such traditional things any longer). There is a future here that is bursting into our now. And it asks of you to bring your own role to mind and for you to stand in its shoes and walk forward."*[171]

I realized today, as this book nears completion that I came to Earth to share this message. Weaving together the sacred teachings and the words of the heroes and way-showers of these times has been possible because of all the people whose work I have drawn from, who in sharing and fulfilling their own roles, enabled me to fulfill my role. It is like a puzzle, with a domino effect as well. When each of us fulfills our role in the Universe's timing, we are able to complete the design and building out of the masterpiece called Love's New Earth. However imperfectly we

---

[171] From It was a Dark and Stormy Night on Planet Earth booklet, by the author, available at https://www.freedomsart.com/offerings

feel we have done, or might be able to do our unique job, **just starting on the path of filling our roles is terrifically important right now.** By creating new systems of education, food production, money exchange, energy production, agriculture, community, water, shelter, communication and more, we will thrive and see our New Earth slowly manifest. If you were to bring your role to mind, and walk forward in its shoes, what would be your next step?

Deborah also had visions of seeing paradise covering the Earth. Once, while in Kentucky, she saw rolling hills and beautiful small family farms and recognized that farms like these would cover the Earth. Another time while standing on the street corner waiting for a bus in St Louis, "Suddenly I am not standing at the bus stop; I am standing in a city that is beyond belief beautiful. There's tall buildings and all the tall buildings are decorated with exquisite mosaic art. There are parks everywhere, water fountains, and air taxis, just like the air cars that are being made now. The main feature in this city was the families: you could *feel the Love* of the moms and dads and the little children. I would see a vision like that, then hear the noise of the bus coming and suddenly I was back in St. Louis. I'd get on, pay my fare and sit down. This kept happening as a very normal activity would shift and suddenly I would see another magnificent, beautiful world."

> We *are* already what it takes to find our way through this time on Earth.

It is rather exciting to realize that these electric air taxis[172] that can go straight up, and fly above the ground are what Deborah saw in 1976, almost 50 years ago. This means we are getting very close to this shift to the New Earth. Holding this vision with Deborah, and imagining (or image-making) places that emanate Love, beauty, artistry, community,

---

[172] https://www.nytimes.com/2023/09/25/business/air-force-joby-electric-air-taxi.html, https://www.flyingmag.com/archers-midnight-electric-air-taxi-completes-inaugural-test-flight/

family and Light in our mind's eye make our future world all the more real and helps us anchor it in this reality, like a blueprint to work from. Let's seek out and support people and groups moving in this direction with us.

Anastasia and Kin's Domains

Wildly successful positive images have been planted by **Anastasia**, a woman now known to millions of people through the *Ringing Cedars of Russia* book series.[173] She lives in the remote Taiga of Siberia, and her purity is beyond our modern-day comprehension. Vladimir Megre met her in 1995 and wrote the books describing her life, her amazing capabilities, perspectives and visions of the future and the past. He also had two children with her. Anastasia helps many people remotely from her woodland glade, by using her "ray" to communicate and inspire them from afar. I too have used my "ray" in a similar way[174] and know that this is possible. Our New Earth is awaiting our inspired engagement with it, using our "rays" is commonplace on the New Earth, and it is something that Anastasia models and shares how to do. You could call it non-local Love, when our Love can touch anything anywhere simply by our focused intent.

Anastasia has also inspired many Eco Villages made up of "Kins Domains" or family homesteads. Kins Domains transform their creators' relationships with plants, animals, each other and the food they eat. They live close to Nature while nurturing the precious next generation, and creating deep bonds with all the life that surrounds them. Kins Domains are not to be taxed and they may be handed down to children, but not sold. Offering this opportunity of a Kins Domain,[175] of one

---

[173] Written by Vladimir Megre about Anastasia, a Russian recluse, millions of copies have been sold in multiple languages.

[174] Mauran, Hope Ives, *Be The Second Coming, Guidebook to the Embodiment of the Christ Within*. The Milosevic Meditations describe a series of Meditative interchanges with Slobodan Milosevic, when he was the President of Yugoslavia. Pgs. 21-26.

[175] Learn more about Kins domains at www Anastasia.Foundation.org https://anastasia.foundation/

hectare (2.47 acres) of land to interested people throughout the world is one way of freeing humanity by enabling them to grow their own food, so they aren't so reliant on current external systems. In Russia all the people are entitled to a Dacha, a plot of land for growing vegetables. Why don't we start by offering a garden plot of 600 square feet to all city dwellers? Many "Dachnics," as they are called by Anastasia, visit their plot on the weekends to work on it, growing healthy and abundant food. In The United States of America, the Homestead Act of 1862 is still in effect, making the claim of land possible if you are resourceful and willing to study what it requires.[176]

The rural self-sufficient life can be physically hard, I am hopeful that we can find ways of living that bridge the ease of our modern lifestyles with new technological innovations, while also reconnecting to Nature, the land, each other, our food and the beauty and abundance of the Earth. I can imagine cities with parks, gardens, greenhouses, fountains and silent non-polluting transportation that all use free energy, a technology that we already have here on Earth, but has been hidden and suppressed.[177] Innovations that we think are just fantasy like anti-gravity devices have been seen by eye witnesses that Stephen Greer's documentaries *The Disclosure Project,* and *The Lost Century* report on. He says that such advanced technologies are already here and being used by a shadow US government. If we can envision these technologies as freely available, their presence here is bound to come. Imagine yourself using them, and distributing them to your friends and neighbors. What an exciting time we live in! What do you want to see in these New Earth communities, and systems? What are you passionate to create?

---

[176] Ron Gibson, a former Marine, has done research on this topic. https://landgrantpatent.org/lectures2.html

[177] National Press Club Event with Dr. Stephen Greer, *Disclosure 2.0,* UFO? UAP Disclosure, June 12, 2023, Documentary on Rumble. He discusses Anti gravity devices and other types of UFO propulsion systems. And in *Thrive 2* by Foster and Kimberly Gamble, they filmed a man and his machine that produced essentially free energy.

Movies, documentaries, podcasts, artwork, billboards, TED talks, songs and other personal and collective uplifting images can seed the New Earth into the here and now. Images, visions and dreams help to inspire us and show us the potential of our world in Love, unity, cooperation, respect for the Earth and nature. Evolved artists, musicians, singers, visionaries and activists are being born on Earth now. Some are precocious high frequency beings of Light. It is up to us to recognize them and support their efforts, as we step up to play our roles, too.

As we become aware of how the darkness has infiltrated our culture, and how chaos, violence, victimhood and a call for safety are being sold by the media, we can make choices to change our focus and thus change our future. What is *wrong* with our world becomes less interesting as we realize that what we focus on will create the world of the future. We can get involved with envisioning it, planning it and building it in groups ourselves.

You never change things by fighting the existing reality. To change something, build a new model that makes the existing model obsolete."
-Buckminster Fuller

CH VIII HUMANITY'S GREATEST OPPORTUNITY

There's an old saying from sports and from the opera: "It ain't over til the fat lady sings." Well folks, the fat lady is now singing. This world we have been previously living in is over. This is the time to turn away and withdraw our support from the old world.

This time has been long awaited. Its uniqueness is that it is the end of a cycle of time and is the time for a great shift.[178] Out of an old way of being on Earth to a new, lighter, more loving opportunity, as the Earth has found her place in a more elevated frequency location. And in many ways it is less of a "fat lady" ending—it's more of a new beginning. A new beginning for the people of Earth as many of us see the missing links of Unity, Love, Interconnection and Cooperation that can hold this world from falling more deeply into separation, disappointment, discouragement and loss. And the ending is a very good thing. The new beginning that it makes space for is to be created here and now, from the metaphorical ashes of the old world structures and systems.

In the same way that a seedling is vulnerable when young, the Earth's New Incarnation needs our help to ensure her successful inflowing of creative energy and Love. And so we can be assured that these words and images that seed Love's New Earth are powerful harbingers of a strong movement in our human family to find our way through this time of massive change. **As we hold focus upon this newly birthed**

---

[178] As mentioned in the overview.

form of Earth, she grows in strength, clarity, stamina, capacity and all due to the (en)visioning of empowered humans who see it is so.

This painting from 2020 shows a seedling Earth being loved and nurtured by a circle of humans holding hands around the base, using their golden heart rays to support its growth.

The key to this successful new beginning is knowing our wholeness, who we *already* are, and thus coming together with respect, cooperation and Love. It is the foundation for healing: to make whole, bringing a fractured human family together with a shared mission is a huge transformational shift. This transformation isn't just a step up; its a quantum shift; it's exponential—it's a 180 degree turn with a step up involved! We can't watch from the sidelines and expect someone else to take care of it. Our clear choice to evolve, awaken, become self responsible and to Love beyond our immediate family (and non-locally) is our next step. Every single one of us matters and has a role to play.

Our role as creators on Earth has been with us all along. Unfortunately we are just a little dinged up and dumbed down and out of practice from having our human DNA[179] and our minds tinkered with over current and historical time. **We have been coerced, herded, molded, schooled, distracted, taxed, poisoned and lured to the situation we find ourselves in. Everything we hold dear is at risk now.** Our old world must phase out; it's extremes are unbalancing the health of the planet, humanity and all life. We need to do some things differently now. **We must stop feeding the old parasitical systems—corporate technocracy, banking systems and pharmaceutical industries—that don't have the same loving vision for the future.** We need to stop focusing on ourselves, and focus upon the creation of our collective home. This transformation is a doorway in time that we don't want to miss, where some of our personal and collective failings that have held us to old patterns and ways can fall away more easily. The Universal wind is at our backs, helping us to leave the old paradigm, freeing us to make the big leap that this shift calls for. We can give each other needed support, strength and encouragement when we envision and work at it together.

> *"Walk ahead one step at a time. Don't give up. Don't worry that you are alone and afraid, others will fall in beside you*

---

[179] Our DNA has been manipulated for various ends. The following quote is from Harald Kautz-Vella's essay in *Dangerous Imagination, Silent Assimilation* by Cara St. Louis; pages 303-319.(Taken from *Geoengineered Transhumanism* by Elana Freeland)"...self-assembling photonic-plasmonic crystals are quantum laser units that take in EM signals and turn them into single photon emissions that communicate with the "DNA." So, electromagnetic signals influence our DNA.

as you walk. This is the gift you have come to offer. It must be given now. It cannot wait. It cannot be put aside for distractions and formulations that are to another master, another end. It is time to march to the light . . . the light and the music within us all." — The Dark and Stormy Night booklet[180]

As we extricate ourselves, we can make a proper home for Love to grow and for the children and families of the New Earth to thrive. The amazingly wonderful thing is we don't have to know exactly how we will do it; *we don't have to figure it all out right away.* That is how the Laws of Nature work. The Field of Love is the fabric into which our visions and ideas are woven, bringing forth synchronicities and miracles

> Don't do unto others what you don't want done to you. -Mark Passio

as our high frequency acknowledges no separation between ourselves and the world. The image we create and hold will manifest when all the necessary steps are fulfilled, and it is for the highest and best good of all concerned. Our work is to stay in alignment with Nature and our Source (and be joyful when we can) (#1), envision only what we do want in physical, energetic or emotional detail(#2), and allow Nature and her team and the Universal Laws to gather the right parts together (#3) to create the actual manifest reality (#4). Synchronicities and miracles are natural when we do our part by focusing on what we *do* want. Keep walking and working towards it as cultivators of harmony. Incorporating stillness into our day, and connecting with Nature helps us to move away from the old patterns that created the old world's problems. Creation is Nature's premier process and we are sanctioned as Creators to create the blueprints for Love's New Earth and build out those blueprints. If we don't who will?

---

[180] From It was a Dark and Stormy Night on Planet Earth booklet, by the author, available at: https://www.freedomsart.com/offerings

Hearts Break Open

As I was editing this chapter on a flight home from Denver, I saw a tiny flash of Light, like a sparkle on the wall, a signal that my higher self has a message for me. I tuned in:

> *In order to facilitate this wholeness, healing and Love-birthed Earth, it requires—no, even demands—a fullness of heart that is not easy for humans to allow (given so much suffering and discord on Earth), and so the coming times of challenge, chaos, tearing down and loss of loved ones will, in a morbid kind of sense, be a great gift in this regard. In such hard times there will come the necessary "heart opening" to allow the fullness to manifest in the hearts, minds and bodies of all humans remaining on Earth. And I feel it is worth noting that this is the case and not to resist its hardship and heart break, but to embrace it in order to free the positive future reality to be born through each of us, from the purity and Love of a humanity cleansed of the created expression of a world built only for personal gain, at the expense of Nature and the Field of Love.*

This is a big one. Embracing instead of resisting our sorrow and sadness is a way to open our hearts more fully. I know that feeling of raw, open, vulnerable Love that we feel at a funeral of a young person who has died too soon or of a close friend or relative. I think it is the final and most precious gift of those who pass on, to break open our hearts. It is from that kind of raw open emptiness that we will be authentic enough to actually create something new and different from the old world. We all have a social crust that keeps our tender egos from being bruised. When that crust of protection breaks open, and perhaps falls away in this higher frequency Earth environment, we stop feeling separate from the world around us, and our wholeness is right there, open and revealed.

How we begin the creation of the New Earth matters. It is like the laying of a cornerstone of a building, or a foundation, that can set the tone for the entire journey to its full creation. So, beginning the creation of the New Earth with an open heart makes the odds of building our creation in that same open hearted condition more likely. Imagine how different our world would be if closed hearts weren't the norm on this Earth. It is not always easy to open our hearts. Most of us don't have any practice in making this shift of opening our heart to other people, life, and the natural world.[181] So if it happens naturally, through grief, or beauty, allow it, and don't resist it in the quest for a "stiff upper lip" or not letting others see you cry.

Ceremony

Eileen, Veronica and I stood in the kitchen tonight, in front of the toasty warm wood stove on a cold dark November evening. I felt a sense of urgency, as a pressure built in my upper chest. My impulse was for the three of us to stand in a circle and hold hands. I didn't know why. We did it, and as we stood there the image of a single point in the center between us arose in my mind. And it came to me that we were seeding the New Earth into the cosmic lattice right there right then in that "spot." It was a spontaneous ceremony that almost created itself.

By my definition, a ceremony anchors something in this world, creates a conversation with Nature, the Consciousness of other forms and the future. It also acknowledges and thanks the team[182] that actually forms our natural world. Robin Wall Kimmerer, a Native American scientist, said that *"Ceremony also reminds us of our responsibilities to creation.[183] Through*

---

[181] The Heartmath Institute has been helping to awaken the heart of humanity for many decades.   https://www.heartmath.org/

[182] By "the team" I am referring to the devas, the energy spirits that help to form material reality. See the Rays of Hope listing on the Findhorn Foundation in the Bibliography for more information.

[183] *The Sun, Two Ways of Knowing,* April 2016 pg 5. with Leath Tonino and Robin Wall Kimmerer.

the ceremony itself—the food, the regalia, the time spent in preparation— you are giving back. You're putting energy back into both the material and spiritual world. The two are inseparable. Ceremonies are as much about reciprocity as they are about gratitude."

Ceremonies often include burning something, a literal and metaphorical transformation or clearing with candles, incense, white sage or ghee. A spoken intention, music, drumming, chanting, movement, honoring, gratitude, worship, prayer and other offerings are a part of them. In ceremonies for Mama Pacha—Mother Earth—I bury chocolate or offer tobacco. Veronica, Eileen and I all spoke our intentions for the New Earth's creation in that ceremony, then allowed the timeless sacred silence to receive them. We then dropped hands and went on with our evening. The ceremony lasted but a few minutes, and left us with a feeling of completion. We had done something that wasn't visible but was still tangible, hopeful and important. Our intention was very real. Envision billions of other humans ceremonially creating and celebrating Love's New Earth, and then organizing their lives around its call.

If the entire human family were to **focus on the same goal**, imagine the natural power we would release in creation!

These few words that inspire the New Earth's creation, and that I think perhaps we can all agree on, are from the book *Becoming*:

> ### *We are creating a New Paradigm on Planet Earth for the Highest and Best Good of All Concerned.*[184]

Repeat that with joy and anticipation for what our New Earth will be like, *feel the goal as already present*. Revel in the *feeling* of it being here right now. Daydream about it. Walk towards it! Take action.

Let's trust that we are here for a reason, and this *is* the time we have all been waiting for! It is no mistake that we are here for the culmination of this cycle of time. Start actively creating now like your life depends

---

[184] *Becoming*, pg .173

on it. Start with ***"I am always in the right place at the right time with the right people,*** [185] ***for the highest and best good of all concerned,"*** and see what unfolds.

Our awareness of our Unity as Consciousness calls all strata of our societies, all levels of humanity to work cooperatively, where we bring our *willingness and our Holiness* together to ensure our successful collaboration, and find new and gentler ways to be in community upon the Earth. Peace is a choice we can and eventually will make.

> Journal entry 1/11/23 -I turn and see the sun rising beneath a chem trail cutting the sky in half towards the east. With my coffee mug on the arm of the chair and the fire warming my feet, I feel gratitude and also the intrusion of these forces that have an agenda that is engineering the weather all over the world.[186] I turn towards the sun and practice a technique called the *Infinity Wave*[187] I trace that infinity form in my mind's eye between my heart and the Sun.[188] It brings peace and harmony and helps me to remember that the Sun too is within me. All is well.

In the way that Lama Rangbar Nyimai Ozer realized "These dogs have nothing to do with me," the weather engineering chemtrails[189] and clouds they seed do not need to divert our attention from creating our new Earth Paradigm; *they cannot truly touch us.* We have a bigger

---

[185] A phrase from Raymon Grace.

[186] https://www.ourgeoengineeringage.org/resources

[187] Hope Fitzgerald's gift of the Infinity Wave is a beautiful, potent and effective practice. whereby I imagine a flowing form of the infinity symbol, which is like a figure 8, going from my heart to the sun and back, over and over... https://www.spreadinfinitehope.com

[188] I am reminded of Kahu Abraham Kawai'i sharing that we generate power when we move our consciousness over long distances. I think it also speeds up and empowers our creative ability.

[189] A resource for books and documentaries on this phenomenon. https://www.ourgeoengineeringage.org/resources

work to attend to. Our creative power is focused instead on creating Love's New Earth and trusting that *everything we need, including the perfect amount of clean air, clear blue sky, sunlight and warmth are present wherever we are, and on Love's New Earth.*

On Love's New Earth children are healthy, emotionally supported, loved, creative, animated, inspired and happy; they are excited for life, learning and living. They are learning the Laws of Nature, how to communicate with all things, how to use their "rays" to help others, and how to investigate the building blocks of this world from within themselves as Consciousness as well as through the sciences, and so much more. I see families and communities supporting each of their member's highest calling. Truly satisfying work and gifting are happening. I see gardens growing healthy, nutrient-dense and abundant food. I feel Earth's sigh of relief and appreciation as her oceans, waters, land and air are clean again. Agriculture, consumption patterns, energy and housing are all in harmony and appropriate reciprocity with Mother Earth. They are designed using Nature's principles. They are healthy, beautiful, unique and comfortable. We can transcend whatever seems to be in our way by coming together as the old world falls apart.

We are creating a New Earth paradigm. Your reading this book has set the wheels of its creation in motion. Look for its evidence now. If you see a piece of it, cheer for it, speak about it, encourage it, support it and help it along. Feel its presence in your heart. Love's New Earth will be envisioned, created and built by us. I imagine when we see the New Earth manifest, bit by bit, day by day, brick by brick, we will wish we had let go of all that stood in its way sooner!

Sarah, who I mentioned in Chapter One, who's package mistakenly came to my porch, successfully gave birth to a baby girl at home, all by herself in five hours on New Year's Eve of 2022. We, too, have successfully given birth... to Love's New Earth. The Covid-19 pandemic started our birthing labor for the New Earth. We have all been in the birth canal these last several years—getting squeezed! It has woken many of us up to our desire and need to live differently. As we leave the darkness and break through into the Light, we are re-born and our New Earth is born with us. As we fill our lungs with air, our cries for Freedom, Love, Unity and Sovereignty are being heard all over the world.

We can now set about making things right with ourselves and each other, and we can nurture the precious New Earth. We are co-Creators of Love's New Earth, and we are creating a **New Earth Paradigm for the highest and best good of all concerned. Love as you would be Loved, give Light as you would like to be Lit, and organize your life to support such things for all beings.** "Small changes in many places and many different occurrences will begin the shift."[190] There is nothing more we need except the courage to begin, the stamina to prevail and the remembrance of the Love within and around us all.

The End

---

[190] *Becoming*, pg 175.

ACKNOWLEDGEMENTS

And infinite love and gratitude to: my guides, higher self, Jesus . . . whose promptings got me to write this book, and who's clarity, guidance and Love are unwavering and still continually surprise me;

Oracle Girl and the Purification Space,[191] she is an inspiration, mirror and role model, who's work ethic and consistent brilliance are amazing, Oracle Girl offers public talks, group & personal purifications entirely by donation. She says: "The future is positive. Dream. Rebuild your societies. Purify yourself and all beings." https://www.oraclegirl.org/.

Jody Fabrikan(t), editor wiz extraordinaire and friend, whose phrasing and language are included here in many places and whose greater clarity, insight, and countless quotes, memes, resources, and ideas have found their way into this book. Her knowledge of these topics has been invaluable, and is so very rare. Our time together on the phone editing live, was often filled with laughter as we tried to reconcile the irreconcilable extremes that this book covers. **And many thanks to** editor John Ferguson who generously volunteered to review the manuscript at the last hour before sending it off for publication. (All remaining errors are mine,) I so enjoyed our work together, and Chris Eldridge for the invaluable computer help, and the team at Balboa press. And Barrie Fisher for her amazing author photo.

Deep gratitude for stories and leads to Ben Schawinsky, Deborah Roberts, Lama Rangbar Nyimai Ozer, RossNewkirk, Marc Newkirk,

---

[191] https://www.oraclegirl.org/glossary

Angela Sumner, Loulie Mauran, Ji Xing Li, Linda Burkhardt, Eileen Duane, Veronica Marr, Sarah Bassin. Dr Richard Warmann and others not mentioned here.

And hats off and a deep bow to all these wise amazing truth tellers, way-showers authors and founders of the New Earth: Anastasia and author Vladimir Megre, Alex Collier, Sadhguru, Dr. David Martin, Matias Desmet, Charles Eisenstein, John Root, Robert Perry, Penny Kelly, Dr Stephen Greer, James Swartz, Swami Svatmananda, Katherine Silvan, Tom Brown, Jr., Robin Wall Kimmerer, Reverend Tony Ponticello, Eriksson Burkholder, Hope Fitzgerald, Stephen and Theresa of the Ownstream Network, Inelia Benz, Amman Jabbi, Machele Small Wright, Gabor Lukacs, Ross and Heather Newkirk, Shane Clairborne, Nicole Matoushek, Jerry Mander, Chris Martenson, PhD, Evie Botelho, Vera Sharav, Foster and Kimberly Carter Gamble, Shane Clairborne, David Icke, Mike Dooley, Anneloes Smitsman, PhD, Josh del Sol, Sayer Ji, Mark Passio, Richard Iadarolla **and many more… thank you, to** *all* **the amazing beings, playing your roles at this pivotal time.**

And gratitude to those pillars of wisdom who have paved our way to here, we stand upon your shoulders… Marc Newkirk, Rudolph Steiner, Mildred Norman Peace Pilgrim, Swami Dyananda Saraswati, Helen Schucman, Bill Thetford, George Greene, Rumi and Kahu Abraham Kawai'i.

May the force be with you, godspeed and deep gratitude to all those listed in the *Rays of Hope and reasons to prevail*, section of this book…who are too many to list here.

I couldn't have done this without the help, friendship, encouragement and perspectives of Eileen and Veronica, who's friendship has been a monumental gift in these times of drastic change, Deborah, who added so much to this story with her visions, and her editing suggestions, Kim for blessing the book upon the mountaintop, and her encouragement as the first to read it through, Suzanne, for her wonderful questions and comments, Katherine, Susan, Loren, Enoka, Monaji, Sarah,

Kristi, Deb, Steve, Diane, Carol, Linda, Ruven, Roy, Tam, Rick, Juan, Melinda, Jesse and Jennifer, and all who read and shared their thoughts I am deeply grateful. And all my inspiring friends at VSU and all my immediate family.

And many thanks to Dr. Grace Johnstone, chiropractor, and visionary who brought Hyperbaric Oxygen Therapy to Montpelier, and the HBOT team, Angela and Erin, I am so very grateful!

And not last in any realm…you the reader and the Field of Love that holds us all. Thank "You."

RAYS OF HOPE AND REASONS TO PREVAIL

This is a sampling of people, ideas and organizations, teaching and demonstrating new ways of living and being, and safeguarding what is good, true and beautiful here on Earth. As we each step into our brilliance, and our unique roles, we can applaud and support those who are already doing some of what needs to be done in order to create Love's New Earth. (As time goes by some links may become invalid, and text in quotation marks is from the listed website for the person or organization.)

Alternative Radio, is "Audio Energy for Democracy. Alternative Radio is an award-winning weekly one-hour public affairs program offered free to all public radio stations in the U.S., Canada, Europe and beyond. AR provides information, analyses, and views that are frequently ignored or distorted in corporate media." https://www.alternativeradio.org/

Anna Breytenbach, is an Animal communicator, who became well known when she communicated with a retired circus animal, a Black Leopard, who for 6 months had angrily refused to go out from its cage on to the open land that it was free to enjoy. After Anna spoke with it, it went out that afternoon. Her website is https://animalspirit.org/

Anneloes Smitsman, PhD., is the author of "Transition Plan for a Thrivable Civilization," from the **EARTHwise Centre,** which in CoCreation with the Four Worlds International Institute, has created a "Constitution for a Planetary Civilization." An excerpt is in the Appendix of Resources. https://www.earthwisecentre.org/

Awaken Wholeness Center, LLC., in Rhode Island, is dedicated to the Awakening and Enlightenment of the Mind, Body, and Spirit, through the use of holistic practices, educational experiences and Consciousness-Raising Technologies for the purpose of empowering humanity to greater health, awareness, and oneness. Director Heather Newkirk is a skilled intuitive. www.AwakenWholenessCenter.com and Ross Newkirk's website: **ConsciousTechnologiesllc.com** offers Conscious raising new technologies and Vogel Crystals for sale.

Building Biology Institute, has a mission to help create healthy homes, schools and workplaces, free of toxic indoor air, tap-water pollutants and hazards posed by electromagnetic radiation. By guiding people to an understanding of the vital and complex interrelationship between the natural and built environments, and teaching them the means for merging these complementary environments into greater harmony and planetary health. The have a directory of certified consultants at https://buildingbiologyinstitute.org/find-an-expert/certified-consultants/

Better Way Conference, "Unveiling a Better Way for Health, Freedom & Sovereignty. "https://betterwayconference.org/

Biodynamics is a holistic, ecological, and ethical approach to farming, gardening, food, and nutrition. https://www.biodynamics.com/what-is-biodynamics

Biogeometry is the science of energy *quality,* developed by **Dr. Ibrahim Karim**, an Egyptian Architect. Biogeometry tools enable "measurement of the quality of the life force of the Earth."[192] Buildings, materials, environments and technology, can be designed to foster health, healing and spiritual upliftment. For example, Biogeometry tools and devices can transform the detrimental quality of cell tower radiation to beneficial for biological life. His most recent book is *Hidden Reality, The BioGeometry Physics of Quality,* The *Science of Subtle Energy and Life Force.* "Paths of knowledge paved with universal truths will illuminate the heart to guide humanity along the *"Way of Universal*

---

[192] Hidden Reality, The Biogeometry Physics of Quality, the science of subtle energy and life force, Dr. Ibrahim Karim, Pg 21, Published 2022 by Dr. Ibrahim F. Karim, Biogeometry Energy Systems LLc.

Unity" that will save the environment." Pg.8. https://www.biogeometry.ca/introduction-to-biogeometry

Bio-nutrient Food Association, works to increase the *quality* of the food supply using enlightened self interest to create more nutrient dense and healthy foods. "We do not fight the forces... that we see as detrimental in the food system, but educate, organize & empower those who understand what it is we're working on." They work with growers, purveyors and consumers and are based in Massachusetts. https://www.bionutrient.org/

Bodhivastu Foundation for Enlightened Activity is committed to the manifestation of an awakened society via the transformation of individuals. "Our energies and activities are dedicated to supporting a quantum awakening to the truth and functionality of our interdependence. Through the implementation of teaching curricula, individual training and practice, preservation and by benevolent projects, through our centers, we work to benefit all beings without exception. Catalyzing Awakening by Individual Transformation, Place and Design. Founded by **Lama Rangbar Nyimai Ozer** who's story I shared in chapter V. **https://www.thegreatawakening.org/**

Branching Out, a high school mentoring program started in Vermont, that matches people in the community with students wishing to learn from them. It has become Big Picture Schools, https://www.bigpicture.org/, and Eagle Rock School and Development Center in Colorado. https://www.eaglerockschool.org/

Catherine Austin Fitts, and her company **Solari** is helping clients to live a free and inspired financial life. This includes building wealth in ways that build real wealth in the wider economy. They publish The Solari Report. https://home.solari.com/about-us/

Charles Eisenstein, an eloquent, soulful, poetic environmentalist is a voice for peace and sanity. Creator of The Sanity Project and author of five books: *Sacred Economics, The Coronation, The More Beautiful World Our Hearts Know Is Possible, The Ascent Of Humanity,* and *The Yoga of Eating.* https://charleseisenstein.org/

Children's Health Defense, has a mission is to end childhood health epidemics by working aggressively to eliminate harmful exposures, hold those responsible accountable and establish safeguards to prevent future harm. We fight corruption, mass surveillance and censorship that put profits before people as well as advocate for worldwide rights to health freedom and bodily autonomy. https://childrenshealthdefense.org/

ClientEarth, uses the power of the law to protect all life on Earth, combining thousands of individual voices into one. They protect wildlife habitats, end pollution, protect forests and more, in the areas of Agriculture, Fisheries, Forests, Air, Clean Energy, Fossil Fuels, Trade, Plastics and Habitat protection. https://www.clientearth.org/

David Hudson, discovered Ormus, "ORME," Orbitally Rearranged Monoatomic Element, a multidimensional substance that can be powerfully beneficial and rejuvenating for the body, mind and spirit. It improves Nitrogen levels in plants, in the soil, in the roots, and improves overall growth. Ormus also improves crop yields, reduces transplant shock, increases drought tolerance, and supports nitrogen fixing bacteria. It also improves soil tilth and aeration, and increased vitamin and mineral content in the crop.[193] It's multidimensionality makes it a very unique substance. https://www.youtube.com/watch?v=0IgYp4Noz90

Daryl Anka, channels **Bashar** a non-physical entity, who's message aligns well with the messages in this book. https://www.bashar.org/

Dr. David Martin, is a Corporate Advisor, Entrepreneur, Financier, Storyteller, Professor and Inventor, "he shows others how to remember what it means to put humanity into the human experience. Over the past 5 decades he's fully lived and has done so in service to humanity. Unlike many who build an identity around accomplishments, he uses his actions to show others the vast extremes of possibility." https://www.davidmartin.world/shop/ The documentary Future Dreaming at https://www.davidmartin.world/future-dreaming/, is inspiring, uplifting and educational.

---

[193] www.WhatIsOrmus.com and www.OrmusMinerals.com, OM By: Ray and Ruth Hamilton, Ormus Minerals Inc. P. O. Box 513, Caldwell, Idaho 83651, an ebook.

Dr. Steven Greer, founder of ***The Disclosure Project,*** which shared first hand accounts of free energy, powering flying objects, which he says the US government has been using in a shadow government for decades [194] He calls for a grassroots effort to have the US Government inquire into the presence of this shadow government and its technologies that have been usurped from the people of the United States and the world. If we all had free energy, it would mean that our houses could be heated and cooled without pollution, it would mean we could heat greenhouses in northern climates to grow ample, healthy food in winter, it would mean pollution-free transportation and so much more. There are forces at work to keep these technologies from being shared, and Dr. Greer is working to untangle the net of control. He also made ***The Lost Century and How To Reclaim It,*** a documentary (available from Amazon), on free energy inventors, and at the end, he illustrates the New Earth that is possible when we share free energy technology with all humanity.

Oracle Girl, offers public talks, group & personal purifications entirely by donation. She says: "The future is positive. Dream. Rebuild your societies. Purify yourself and all beings." https://www.oraclegirl.org/.

Dr. Joe Dispenza, is a neuroscientist, researcher, chiropractor, author and inspiring international lecturer who educates people on how to rewire their brains to use their full creative potential. He offers workshops, meditations and books on reconditioning bodies and exercising the mind. https://drjoedispenza.com/

Earthships: "is a style of architecture developed in the late 20th century to early 21st century by architect Michael Reynolds. Earthships are designed to behave as passive solar earth shelters made of both natural and upcycled materials such as earth-packed tires. Earthships may feature a variety of amenities and aesthetics, and are designed to withstand the extreme temperatures of a desert, managing to stay close to 70 °F (21 °C) regardless of outside weather conditions." (From Wikipedia) https://en.wikipedia.org/wiki/Earthship

---

[194] National Press Club Event with Dr Steven Greer, Disclosure 2.0, UFO / UAP Disclosure, June 12, 2023, on Rumble.

Epoch Times Association is dedicated to seeking the truth through insightful and independent journalism, standing outside of political interests and the pursuit of profit, in order to serve the public benefit and be truly responsible to society. https://www.theepochtimes.com/about-us#our-story

EWG Skin Deep, learn what's really in your personal care products. https://www.ewg.org/skindeep/

Farm Match. Com, is creating a decentralized, regenerative, food system, where buyers and farmers can get connected. Just put your zip code into the search bar, to locate nearby farms. https://www.farmmatch.com/search?q= In addition, the **Westin A. Price Foundation** https://www.westonaprice.org/#gsc.tab=0 has lists of local farmers to buy from.

Findhorn Foundation In 1962, David and Eileen Caddy, their two children and Dorothy, a friend, moved into a trailer park on a windswept sandy Scottish shoreline. They planted a garden and later began communicating with the devas, the elementals and the nature spirits, largely out of necessity to grow food. The communication led to a partnership with the hidden conscious energies that form the structure of the physical world, and a magnificent garden resulted. *The Findhorn Garden, Pioneering a New Vision of Man and Nature in Cooperation,* by the Findhorn Community. It's foreword, by William Irwin Thompson, is one of several books dedicated to "an exploration of the newly emerging planetary society and the future evolution of man."[195]

Foster and Kimberly Carter Gamble, started the **Free to Thrive** movement. *Thrive, Thrive II: This Is What It Takes*, is a must watch documentary in order to know what it takes to create a new kind of Earth, it chronicles a search for and the discovery of a free energy device and he discovers one made by a man in Africa. With free energy, the entire game is changed on Earth. Foster's much needed *Declaration of Ethics for Artificial Intelligence* is included in the resources appendix. https://www.youtube.com/watch?v=nq2MCxXn3vg

---

[195] 1975, the Findhorn Foundation

Gaia Foundation is re-weaving the basket of life with food and seed sovereignty, moving beyond extractivism, supporting earth jurisprudence, sacred lands and waters. https://gaiafoundation.org

Gaia TV, "is the largest online resource for consciousness-expanding videos." They offer documentaries, films, series and classes, for a membership fee. https://www.gaia.com/

The Goldback® is the world's first physical, interchangeable, gold money, that is designed to accommodate small transactions. https://www.goldback.com/

Gregg Braden "is a five-time New York Times best-selling author, scientist, international educator and renowned as a pioneer in the emerging paradigm based in science, social policy and human potential." https://greggbraden.com/

Gwendolyn Awen Jones is "an award-winning author known for her books on healing and spirituality. She was born with a natural gift of spiritual sight that allows her to see the subtle energies beyond the normal physical world.... She has trained to use her spiritual gifts for healing others." https://angelsoflightandhealing.org/

Harald Kautz-Vella, is an independent scientific researcher based in Germany. His revealing work is founded on biophoton research and scalar physics. His story, which starts with hard-core chemistry and physics, exposes the hidden agenda of the anti-natural assimilation of all natural life forms on this planet, and at the end, towards spiritual transcendence. https://www.youtube.com/watch?v=pq3b6R7_M4g

Harry Uhane Jim, Kahuna, healer, teacher. Author of *WISE SECRETS OF ALOHA,* Harry was trained in the traditional apprentice style by the best known native Kahunas of the last 7 decades. His presentations carry authenticity and are known for unveiling profound ancient truths with wit and laughter. http://www.harryjimlomilomi.com/10385.html

Healing Technologies, listed here for *you* to investigate, I am not promoting them, just sharing my awareness that they exist: **EES:** https://eesystem.com/eesystem/ **Radionics:** https://radionics.us/ **Rife**

Machines, Med Beds, A New Cancer Treatment: https://histosonics.com/our-technology/ called https://www.sciencealert.com/scientists-destroy-99-of-cancer-cells-in-the-lab-using-vibrating-molecules

HeartMath Institute's mission is "to co-create a kinder, more compassionate world by conducting interconnectivity research and providing heart-based, science-proven tools for raising humanity's baseline consciousness from separation and discord to compassionate care and cooperation." https://www.heartmath.org/

Hope Fitzgerald, Founder of the Wave Energy Center for Conscious Evolution, received a series of visions in 2010, which culminated into a watery, flowing figure "8." This moving geometry is a 10th-dimensional energetic tool called the Infinity Wave sent to us by a benevolent Universe for upcoming tumultuous times (which are upon us now). Hope's mission is to encourage individual and planetary awakening around the globe. https://www.linkedin.com/in/hope-fitzgerald-05664619

Inelia Benz, says that she had she "never incarnated on Earth before and she had never incarnated in the Universe before. She came straight out of creation and into a physical body elemental who, thankfully, was well versed and highly experienced in expressing physically on Earth. She was born free from self-importance, attachments, personal agendas, and free from the desire to evolve either physically or soul-wise. She has worked tirelessly to explore, investigate, develop, and disseminate tools, including meditations and exercises that are quick, mystery-free and highly effective — tools used to raise the vibrational frequency of the planet." https://walkwithmenow.com/ https://ineliabenz.com/

Institute of Integrated Regenerative Design, Allan Booker, is the founder and executive director who "trains professional design practitioners to create systems that are ecosystemic, biocompatible and regenerative. In addition to teaching Permaculture and Integrated Regenerative Design, the Institute also provides consulting and workshops on earthworks, watershed management, soil remediation, composting, forest gardening, holistic management of pastureland, keyline design, aquaculture and aquaponics, Net Zero buildings, off-grid energy systems, and natural building systems." https://learn.i2rd.co/

Institute of Noetic Sciences, they fund the **Global Consciousness Project,** "Through modern scientific inquiry, we seek to better understand a timeless truth that humanity is deeply interconnected." https://noetic.org/

John Root,[196] studied the systems of life from outside of the mainstream for decades. His *Natural Law Jural assembly Communities* are based upon everyone's active consent, the desire of the individual to be free in a just society, with collaboration in an economy and currency that benefits everyone. Our current monetary system enriches the banking system, John's model enriches the community that supports it. The only law is Do No Harm. Look for his book on the website: https://www.justabundance.org/
This link to Imagining to Manifesting is worth reading: https://docs.google.com/document/d/1o5f3miTB6IFe9GI7yyxrO1Fzenled2SOMDeoApRfG1Q/edit

Josh del Sol and Sayer Ji 5G Crisis, and hosts of the 5G Crisis Summit, interviewed 40 of the world's leading PhD, legal experts, researchers and public safety advocates. https://archive.org/details/the_5g_crisis_summit_2019_audio_only

Jude Currivan, PhD., "Our purpose is to empower our conscious evolution through the understanding, experiencing and embodying of unitive awareness." It "offers the latest unitive scientific breakthroughs, evidence of a conscious and evolutionary Universe, and fellow communities, networks, tools and examples of how we can understand, experience and embody unitive awareness." www.wholeworld-view.org

Keep Cash Alive, a push to maintain physical cash currency worldwide, which supports businesses instead of banks and large corporations. www.keepcashalive.com

Lightfield Foundation, created by **Marc Newkirk**, and a team of intuitives helps people connect to higher levels of their consciousness

---

[196] Natural law and Human Nature LIVE interview of Joh Root. 3/16/23, Governing Ourselves Podcast, Joe Charter, Rumble.com, #infowindnewnews

using a coherent field that helps one shed energy distortions at all levels. https://www/lightfieldfoundation.com

Local Harvest.Org, connects you to farms, farmers markets, CSA's, restaurants, Co-ops, U-Pick, farm stands, wholesale and meat processors. You can use this website to start a local food buying club too. https://www.localharvest.org/locations/

Marine Conservation Institute, "is dedicated to securing permanent, strong protection for the oceans" the most important places for us and for future generations… They are focusing on protection of whole marine ecosystems… They are creating Blue Parks, marine protected areas for biodiversity protection." https://marine-conservation.org/

Michael Tellinger, is a "scientist, author, researcher, explorer, activist, humanitarian and founder of the Ubuntu Liberation Movement." His books are: *UBUNTU Contributionism, A Blueprint for Human Prosperity* and *Speaking into Existence*: *The Power of Vowels and the Science of Attraction.* https://www.michaeltellinger.com/ This 25 min. video illustrates the power of sound and voice. https://www.youtube.com/watch?v=Ij8T1QCPY7I.

Mission Darkness, is made "by MOS Equipment, is a global leader in radio frequency (RF) shielding solutions. "Our product range includes mobile device analysis enclosures, shielded lockers, and specially designed faraday bags, all tailored for the secure handling of digital devices." ushttps://mosequipment.com/pages/about-us

Moolacoins from "Helios Farms, a group of farms that share an ethic and have created a milk-backed monetary system." A model that others might be inspired by. New currencies are one way to support local autonomy and economies. https://www.heliosfarms.com/product-page/moolacoin

Marjory Wildcraft and The Grow Network, a community of people and expert speakers focused on modern self-sufficient living. https://thegrownetwork.com/

NonViolent Communication, is a "way of being in the world that has the purpose to serve life and to create connection in such a way that everyone's needs can be met through natural care." It is a way of asking questions, holding space and creating dialogue between people, it builds bridges between impossibly separated viewpoints and individuals. Developed by Marshall Rosenberg. https://www.cnvc.org/

Organic Consumers Association, "a non profit, US-based network of more than two million consumers dedicated to safeguarding organic standards and promoting a healthy, just and regenerative system of food, farming, and commerce." Ronnie Cummins is its founder and director. https://organicconsumers.org/about/

Peace Pilgrim, Mildred Norman. Her Friends of Peace Pilgrim organization, sends out a free book to anyone who is interested in her life and writings which inspire peace on Earth. https://www.peacepilgrim.org/about-us

Peak Prosperity, "The #1 Resilience Community," founded by Chris Martenson, PhD., an economic researcher and futurist specializing in energy and resource depletion, author of *The Crash Course, an honest approach to facing the future of our economy, energy, and environment.* https://peakprosperity.com/

Penny Kelly, author of *The Revival- Path to A New Earth/New Human* is a handbook for transforming our present level of consciousness. It educates us to the level where we might live on this Earth in peace and in communion with Nature and each other. It requires us to deeply talk to each other and to dredge our minds and hearts for our true desires and values. It asks of us to take stock of what we are (and are not) doing and "what we could be doing and *must be doing.*" Penny's experiences with off-planet beings, and their perspectives on humanity, help to shape her vision of where we need to be going on a New Earth. Why not start a study group of this book in your community, or make this book part of a high school or college curriculum? https://pennykelly.com/

Permaculture, integrates land, resources, people and the environment through mutually beneficial synergies – imitating the no waste, closed loop systems seen in diverse natural systems. Permaculture studies and applies holistic solutions that are applicable in rural and urban contexts at any scale. https://www.permaculturenews.org/what-is-permaculture/

Privacy Academy with Glen and Eric Meder. Online privacy guides, classes and more. https://privacyacademy.com/

Private Membership Associations, "PMA, A Private Membership Association is men and woman collectively asserting and standing upon their secured perfect rights to assemble and associate; their reserved authority; their pre-existing claim to absolute authority and control over the health of their own body, mind, spirit and rights. A "PMA" functions by the members acting as Men and Women in their real private character and capacity. "No State can make a law that impairs the obligation of a contract and therefore is without jurisdiction." https://pmapower.org/about/

Raymon Grace Foundation, Raymon Grace is a master dowser. His foundation's mission "is to educate people throughout the world on how to clean up water and be able to provide clean, drinkable water for their families and their communities." He has taught many how to dowse at a very advanced level. When people ask him if something is possible he responds "try it." He is a champion of everyone's power to create, transform and mitigate what they don't like in their environment. https://www.raymongracefoundation.org/

Sacha Stone, articulate, truth teller, "former rock musician, shock poet activist, public speaker, publisher, writer and filmmaker. He established **Humanitad** in 1999 and is an outspoken advocate of human rights and natural justice, founding the International Tribunal for Natural Justice in 2015. He has instigated judicial commissions for thousands of residents committed to planetary emancipation." Www.sachastone.com

Sociocracy, is a governance system, just like democracy or corporate governance methods, and is best suited for organizations that want to self-govern based on the values of equality, it is suitable for communities and other organizations. https://www.sociocracyforall.org/sociocracy/ https://www.sociocracyforall.org/sociocracy/

Slim Sperling, was "an artist, scientist and inventor. He created the first Light-Life Ring in 1991." His inventions are used for health improvement, reducing air pollution, improving plant growth, restoring soil and water, and reducing pesticide use. His devices cleared the pollution from Denver Colorado in an hour, (a story told in the book *Slim Spurling's Universe*, by Cal Garrison). His wife Katharina continues to make his devices available. https://lightlifetechnology.com/

Teach Communication with Nature Spirits for gardeners, foresters, geologists and others who interact with nature and her "resources." We can develop new ways of communicating and supporting each other, an idea for a niche that you might fill on the New Earth.

The American Society of Dowsers, is a non-profit organization that disseminates knowledge of dowsing (water witching, the discovery of lost articles or persons, and related para-psychological phenomena). https//dowsers.org/

The Law For Mankind Knowledge Share, "Discover How To Set Your Law To Govern Your Life, So You Can Live Life On Your Terms Without Giving Away Yourself, Your Property Or Your Rights To Anyone Ever Again." https://thesovereignsway.com/courses/ Classes that teach you the Law of the True Earth, in contrast to the legal system.

The Ocean Cleanup, Boylan Slat went scuba diving when he was 15 and saw more plastic bags than fish, and thought, "why can't we just clean this up?" His organization is cleaning the oceans and developing additional ocean cleaning technologies. Their mission is to rid the world's oceans of plastic and trash. https://theoceancleanup.com/

The Secret Life of Plants, by Peter Thompkins and Christopher Bird is a book from the 1960's that chronicles how police detective placed a lie detector device on a plant, only to discover plants to be sentient, and able to communicate with humans. This book ought to be studied in schools and universities everywhere.

TimeBanks.org, TimeBanking is a unique way of building community through trust, where members depend on one another. You can earn credits by giving your time to help someone and then spending those earned credits receiving help in return. Everyone's time is valued equally and one hour you give = one hour credit earned. https://timebanks.org/

Tom Brown, Jr., and The Tracker School, "a renowned tracker, teacher, and author. When Tom was only seven, Stalking Wolf (Grandfather), a Southern Lipan Apache elder, shaman and scout, began coyote teaching Tom in the skills of tracking, wilderness survival, and awareness. After Stalking Wolf's final walk, Tom spent the next ten years wandering the wilderness throughout the America's with no manufactured tools-in most cases not even a knife-perfecting these Grandfathers skills and teachings." The school teaches a closer connection to the Earth, and the outdoor survival skills and philosophy that helps us remember harmony and balance with Creation. The classes teach a reverence for life and the land, and the spirit that moves through all things. www.trackerschool.com

Tom has taught many fine teachers who also share Grandfather's wisdom and skills including **Rick Berry of 4EEE: Four Elements Earth Education,** https://www.4eee.org/

TreeSisters, "our vision is to ethically expand the green cover of our world and our mission is to work in harmony with trees and their communities, for the planet to survive and thrive. Projects protect endangered species, empower communities, reforest lands and create greenways for wildlife." https://www.treesisters.org/

United Plant Savers, "For the research, education, and conservation of native medicinal plants, fungi, and their habitats." https://unitedplantsavers.org/

Vandana Shiva, Indian physicist and author of *Terra Viva*, scientist, activist and protector of biodiverse systems. She founded the **Research Foundation for Science, Technology, and Natural Resource Policy** (RFSTN), an organization devoted to developing sustainable methods of agriculture. https://navdanyainternational.org/our-staff/vandana-shiva/

Veda Austin, "is a water researcher, public speaker, mother, artist and author. She has dedicated the last 10 years observing and photographing the life of water. She believes that water is fluid intelligence, observing itself through every living organism on the planet and in the Universe. She photographs of water in its "state of creation,' the space between liquid and ice. It is through her remarkable crystallographic photos that water reveals its awareness of not only Creation, but thought and intention through imagery. Veda brings a message of hope and joy from the very source of life itself. She says "Water is transparent, it knows no color, creed or religion. Water does not judge, nor does it label, it will enter the body of an ant as easily as it will enter the body of a king, or a homeless person or a tree or a dragonfly." https://www.vedaaustin.com/

Vedanta Teachers, are a necessary aspect for truly receiving this means of knowledge of who we are as Consciousness. Some Vedanta teachings are mentioned in this book.

James Swartz, teacher, and author of many books including: *The Essence of Enlightenment*, Vedanta, TheScience of Consciousness.,https://www.shiningworld.com,

Swami Svatmananda, a modern-day teacher who was successful in the business world, prior to donning the orange robes and choosing the path of a teacher of Vedanta. He resides at an ashram in Saylorsbug, Pennsylvania, and teaches in Europe as well. Http://www.svaaji.com

Swami Paramarthananda: A teacher of teachers, his recordings are filled with spiritual joy and great clarity. Recordings available at the Arsha Vidya Ashram book store in Pennsylvania. https://www.avgbooks.org/

Viktor Schauberger (1885-1958), a Swiss forester from a long line of foresters. His "abiding interest was to discover how to generate energy using Nature's own methods."[197] Victor observed how fish can swim upstream with little effort due to the movement of water around their gills, creating a negative pressure zone as the water flows past the fish, and thus accelerates its ability to stay in place in the moving water. His keen observations inspired many generator designs and nature based solutions to human problems. Victor coined the term "**Biologically**

---

[197] Hidden Nature, the startling insights of Viktor Schauberger, by Alick Bartholomew

Oriented Technology."[198] He observed that Nature uses implosion for energy generation, and humanity uses explosion. Implosion generates 127% more energy than explosion.[199] The opposite of explosion (which expands the volume), implosion reduces the volume occupied and *concentrates* matter *and* energy."

Wireless Education, Ceci Doucette, founder and Education Services Director with the international non-profit, which has distilled the independent scientific literature and medical advisories into affordable 30-minute on-line courses for Schools, Families and Corporate Safety Instruction. wirelesseducation.org

---

[198] Hidden Nature, the startling insights of Viktor Schauberger, by Alick Bartholomew, pg. 266.
[199] HidHidden Nature, the startling insights of Viktor Schauberger, by Alick Bartholomew, pg 249.

APPENDIX OF RESOURCES

Declaration of Ethics for Artificial Intelligence from Foster Gamble
https://www.freetothrive.com/blog/declaration-of-ethics-for-artificial-intelligence/

Introduction and Context: The computer era has made much of life more efficient and more organized for humankind.

The next step in this realm has been the introduction of Artificial Intelligence, or AI — computers and robotic entities that can perform many human tasks, including learning and decision making. To date, we have seen the benefits of this in situations such as assembly lines and medical procedures, and we are now on the cusp of that same technology making possible the production of robots for the purpose of controlling society.

We are at risk of seeing a loss of human freedom and even a loss of what makes us human, like genuine compassion, wonder, vision, intuition and love.

While AI can be helpful, it is, by definition and by the intent of its creators, capable of developing beyond the control of its original programmers. This capacity to gain skills outside of those originally programmed and beyond those of humans is in fact the goal of many of its primary funders and incubators. This is called "The Singularity." Along with the limitations of human consciousness and biased values that program the AI, this leaves open the question as to whether a code of ethics, a "moral compass," will be instituted that will control the algorithms and robots. If we are to enjoy the benefits of AI while eliminating or minimizing the risks, we need clarity on and a means to enforce such a code.

This Declaration of Ethical AI is intended to establish that code.

Non-Aggression Principle (NAP)

Ethical behavior by humankind is based upon the non-initiation of force or fraud toward others and their property. This is known as the Non-Aggression Principle (NAP). We assert that it is essential that no robot be created without this principle being programmed as a central guide to its function — regardless of place, time, culture, community, gender, race, age or condition.

Vital Distinctions Underlying This Declaration

Morality is the practical day-to-day application of universal and rational ethical theories. It is analogous to the relationship between engineering and physics.

Coherent ethical guidelines cannot impose positive (pro-active) moral obligations upon people (i.e. THOU SHALT, as opposed to THOU SHALT NOT), because that requires coercion, which is a violation of the NAP. Thus, rational ethics can only be *protective,* i.e. outlining boundaries that can be justly enforced, rights that can be morally defended. This starts with the recognition that we each own our own bodies, the fruits of our labor, and our rightfully gained property.

Rightfully gained property is created or acquired through original development (like homesteading unowned property or original intellectual property), purchase, trade, gift or inheritance.

Positive (proactive) moral virtues, such as courage, generosity, friendliness, compassion and humor can be promoted, encouraged and modeled, but they cannot be imposed or enforced. Positive moral traits and behavior are only a value when they are freely chosen.

Honoring differences in culture, religious beliefs, sexual preferences etc. is ethical only as long as the NAP is upheld and individuals are not being violated.

Many so-called "Transhumanists" dream of turning over planet Earth to robots and computers. They are beginning by merging digital devices with our organic biology. They have struggled unsuccessfully to get consciousness and life from digital calculation. Ethical AI can help lift our quality of life but it can never and should never replace our sacred purpose to evolve our living consciousness, learn how to love one another, steward our natural environment and live in harmony with the cosmos that is our home.

Examples of What We Cannot Ethically Have in Artificial Intelligence:

Covert or deceptive terms of service. (Fraud)

Theft of personal data. (Stealing)

Withholding of information that is critical to informed consent. (Fraud)

Forced, mandated or covert implants, injections or aerosolization of nanobots. (Invasion of body)

Programming AI to violate the Non-Aggression Principle in any way. (Automated immorality has the capacity to affect many billions of people without recourse or consequence and has no consciousness to motivate its reflection or change.)

Anything that imposes an unknown or unacceptable risk for those potentially impacted; for example (but not necessarily limited to): contamination or destruction by nuclear radiation, gain of function[200] bioweapons etc. (Assault / murder)

---

[200] "Gain of function" refers to the manipulation of DNA in order to gain a function that is not present in an organism. This sentence in Wikipedia is rather revealing of what some researchers are working on. "The term "gain of function" is sometimes applied more narrowly to refer to "research which could enable a pandemic-potential pathogen to replicate more quickly or cause more harm in humans or other closely-related mammals."[5][6] https://en.wikipedia.org/wiki/Gain-of-function_research

Censorship of free speech (Theft of bodily autonomy, since the products of one's labor — words — are eliminated without permission. (The courts must determine the limits of speech, such as incitement to violence, slander, libel etc.)

Poisoning of air, water, food, people. (Assault / murder)

Declaration of Ethics for Artificial Intelligence

The Non-Aggression Principle (NAP), the core of all human ethics, recognizes that no person has the right to initiate force, coercion, or fraud against another — except in true self-defense. Artificial Intelligence (AI) must be subject to the same code of ethics as humankind itself.

Such restrictions on Artificial Intelligence shall include, but not necessarily be limited to:

Assault, Theft Rape Murder Fraud Trespass Destruction of property (including data and intellectual property) Censorship Violation of Informed Consent

All the above protections are understood under this Declaration to be the natural and equal rights of all individual persons, regardless of race, gender, religion, nationality or ethnicity. All AI shall notify every individual if anything is being done to them contrary to their stated will. All AI programs and robots are to be created and applied in accordance with this Declaration.

https://www.freetothrive.com/blog/declaration-of-ethics-for-artificial-intelligence/?utm_source=ONTRAPORT-email-campaign&utm_medium=ONTRAPORT-email-campaign&utm_term=&utm_content=Read+Foster%27s+Declaration+of+Ethics+for+Artificial+Intelligence&utm_campaign=230521-Email

* * * * * * * * * * * * *

Jesus is one of my spirit guides, here is his Commentary of the Resurrection. The Resurrection is the finest example of a freedom-from-the-body story I can think of. It occurs to me to ask him to tell it for us here.

> *Dear One, it was a story that is momentous in human history, for it did in complete trust diffuse the embankment that humanity had built around the body. It changed what is possible for the human family. By transcending the body's experience so fully, and returning to see and speak with my friends, the entire opportunity was shifted for humanity, away from the iteration of selfhood as body bound, to a free and light filled emanation of who I am before and within the body. When I said and "you shall do greater" I meant it. I thought many would be able to follow my lead in this. Now as the frequency of the Earth has risen, it is easier for you all to transcend (the body) and embody the purest divine Love and Light that you are capable of. It is a frequency so high that the body doesn't need to be present anymore. Yet, even as a human in form and body, there is much opportunity to demonstrate miracles and other seeming aberrations from this set of structures that hold this reality together. And so I invite your practical application of this knowledge to bring true freedom to your soul and system of Life. You see, you aren't strictly an individual, you could call yourself a system of Life, that is influencing all the Life around you. Imagine what might happen as many humans learned their true identity as Love incarnate, as the Christ or Divine Principle… while in the body and on Earth. What a beautiful opportunity is right here and now. As you well know, there is much that stands in the way of this, historically, culturally, in education and governmental intrusion to the lives of individuals. Nonetheless it is possible, and the world awaits more and more of you, willing and focused singularly upon this opportunity… not for personal freedom, but to*

> *demonstrate to all the human family the innate freedom of the one who you Truly Are ... the comprehensive freedom that is possible from this knowledge.*

Jesus, it is said, traveled to India[201] and learned the knowledge of who he was. His command of it was complete in his demonstration of the resurrection of his body after the experience on the cross. You may take this as a metaphor for the path that may illustrate who we actually are. I don't mean at all to suggest that suffering and pain are required on our path, just that a singular focus on who we are beyond the body frees us from the situations we find ourselves in on Earth.

* * * * * * * * * * * * * *

Purification and the Purification Space Definitions from OracleGirl.org (https://www.oraclegirl.org/glossary)

Purification. Something you receive from your own source connection via your own self healing ability. A moment of pure love experienced in time and space. A stimulus and realignment to further embody your own purity, which automatically switches on your own ability to purify and self heal.

Purification space. Love made real. The space within you where patterns and blocks naturally fall away. Area within you which transmutes and deletes the setting of the slave self for all beings. The faculty you already have to transmute your family patterns and personal issues - as well as free your ancestors and family line. Also offered externally by myself, for all beings, as a manifestation of the internal frequency of pure love you already operate at. The material field of the purity of your own being. Total, cumulative frequency of purification potential currently available on the planet.

* * * * * * * * * * * * * *

---

[201] Jesus Lived In India, by Holger Kersten, Jesus Lived in India: His Unknown Life Before and After the Crucifixion, 2001.

The Declaration of Independence: In Congress, July 4, 1776

The unanimous Declaration of the thirteen united States of America, When in the Course of human events, it becomes necessary for one people to dissolve the political bands which have connected them with another, and to assume among the powers of the earth, the separate and equal station to which the Laws of Nature and of Nature's God entitle them, a decent respect to the opinions of mankind requires that they should declare the causes which impel them to the separation.

We hold these truths to be self-evident, that all men are created equal, that they are endowed by their Creator with certain unalienable Rights, that among these are Life, Liberty and the pursuit of Happiness.— That to secure these rights, Governments are instituted among Men, deriving their just powers from the consent of the governed, —That whenever any Form of Government becomes destructive of these ends, it is the Right of the People to alter or to abolish it, and to institute new Government, laying its foundation on such principles and organizing its powers in such form, as to them shall seem most likely to effect their Safety and Happiness. Prudence, indeed, will dictate that Governments long established should not be changed for light and transient causes; and accordingly all experience hath shewn, that mankind are more disposed to suffer, while evils are sufferable, than to right themselves by abolishing the forms to which they are accustomed. But when a long train of abuses and usurpations, pursuing invariably the same Object evinces a design to reduce them under absolute Despotism, it is their right, it is their duty, to throw off such Government, and to provide new Guards for their future security.—Such has been the patient sufferance of these Colonies; and such is now the necessity which constrains them to alter their former Systems of Government. The history of the present King of Great Britain is a history of repeated injuries and usurpations, all having in direct object the establishment of an absolute Tyranny over these States. To prove this, let Facts be submitted to a candid world.

He has refused his Assent to Laws, the most wholesome and necessary for the public good.

He has forbidden his Governors to pass Laws of immediate and pressing importance, unless suspended in their operation till his Assent should be obtained; and when so suspended, he has utterly neglected to attend to them.

He has refused to pass other Laws for the accommodation of large districts of people, unless those people would relinquish the right of Representation in the Legislature, a right inestimable to them and formidable to tyrants only.

He has called together legislative bodies at places unusual, uncomfortable, and distant from the depository of their public Records, for the sole purpose of fatiguing them into compliance with his measures.

He has dissolved Representative Houses repeatedly, for opposing with manly firmness his invasions on the rights of the people.

He has refused for a long time, after such dissolutions, to cause others to be elected; whereby the Legislative powers, incapable of Annihilation, have returned to the People at large for their exercise; the State remaining in the mean time exposed to all the dangers of invasion from without, and convulsions within.

He has endeavoured to prevent the population of these States; for that purpose obstructing the Laws for Naturalization of Foreigners; refusing to pass others to encourage their migrations hither, and raising the conditions of new Appropriations of Lands.

He has obstructed the Administration of Justice, by refusing his Assent to Laws for establishing Judiciary powers.

He has made Judges dependent on his Will alone, for the tenure of their offices, and the amount and payment of their salaries.

He has erected a multitude of New Offices, and sent hither swarms of Officers to harrass our people, and eat out their substance.

He has kept among us, in times of peace, Standing Armies without the Consent of our legislatures.

He has affected to render the Military independent of and superior to the Civil power.

He has combined with others to subject us to a jurisdiction foreign to our constitution, and unacknowledged by our laws; giving his Assent to their Acts of pretended Legislation:

For Quartering large bodies of armed troops among us:

For protecting them, by a mock Trial, from punishment for any Murders which they should commit on the Inhabitants of these States:

For cutting off our Trade with all parts of the world:

For imposing Taxes on us without our Consent:

For depriving us in many cases, of the benefits of Trial by Jury:

For transporting us beyond Seas to be tried for pretended offences

For abolishing the free System of English Laws in a neighbouring Province, establishing therein an Arbitrary government, and enlarging its Boundaries so as to render it at once an example and fit instrument for introducing the same absolute rule into these Colonies:

For taking away our Charters, abolishing our most valuable Laws, and altering fundamentally the Forms of our Governments:

For suspending our own Legislatures, and declaring themselves invested with power to legislate for us in all cases whatsoever.

He has abdicated Government here, by declaring us out of his Protection and waging War against us.

He has plundered our seas, ravaged our Coasts, burnt our towns, and destroyed the lives of our people.

He is at this time transporting large Armies of foreign Mercenaries to compleat the works of death, desolation and tyranny, already begun with circumstances of Cruelty & perfidy scarcely paralleled in the most barbarous ages, and totally unworthy the Head of a civilized nation.

He has constrained our fellow Citizens taken Captive on the high Seas to bear Arms against their Country, to become the executioners of their friends and Brethren, or to fall themselves by their Hands.

He has excited domestic insurrections amongst us, and has endeavoured to bring on the inhabitants of our frontiers, the merciless Indian Savages, whose known rule of warfare, is an undistinguished destruction of all ages, sexes and conditions.

In every stage of these Oppressions We have Petitioned for Redress in the most humble terms: Our repeated Petitions have been answered only by repeated injury. A Prince whose character is thus marked by every act which may define a Tyrant, is unfit to be the ruler of a free people.

Nor have We been wanting in attentions to our Brittish brethren. We have warned them from time to time of attempts by their legislature to extend an unwarrantable jurisdiction over us. We have reminded them of the circumstances of our emigration and settlement here. We have appealed to their native justice and magnanimity, and we have conjured them by the ties of our common kindred to disavow these usurpations, which, would inevitably interrupt our connections and correspondence. They too have been deaf to the voice of justice and of consanguinity. We must, therefore, acquiesce in the necessity, which denounces our Separation, and hold them, as we hold the rest of mankind, Enemies in War, in Peace Friends.

We, therefore, the Representatives of the united States of America, in General Congress, Assembled, appealing to the Supreme Judge of the world for the rectitude of our intentions, do, in the Name, and by Authority of the good People of these Colonies, solemnly publish and declare, That these United Colonies are, and of Right ought to be Free and Independent States; that they are Absolved from all Allegiance to the British Crown, and that all political connection between them and the State of Great Britain, is and ought to be totally dissolved; and that as Free and Independent States, they have full Power to levy War, conclude Peace, contract Alliances, establish Commerce, and to do all other Acts and Things which Independent States may of right do. And for the support

of this Declaration, with a firm reliance on the protection of divine Providence, we mutually pledge to each other our Lives, our Fortunes and our sacred Honor. https://www.archives.gov/founding-docs/declaration-transcript

* * * * * * * * * * * * *

THE GREAT RESET (AGENDA 2030) IN A NUTSHELL

In a nutshell, the global plan is comprehensive, aggressive and well organized, and the intention is to significantly reduce the population on Earth,[202] and turn the remaining humans into soul-less machines.[203]

An infrastructure is being built out now to enforce the globalists' control plans, all over the world. The proliferation of surveillance cameras everywhere, including inside your car, is so that we might all be identified with facial recognition and physical biometric software, tracked, monitored and controlled,[204] via Artificial Intelligence and monitored in centralized hubs. A social credit score that ranks our actions is designed to determine what we are able to do. If we do as the central authority wants, we get privileges and can access life's basic needs. If we don't do what the central authority wants, our ability to buy food, travel, go to doctors or hospitals, restaurants and public buildings, and our spending power, may be eliminated. As part of their plan, cash would be removed from the exchange system, all banking and all transactions may go digital with the issuing of Central Bank Digital Currency (CBDCs). Centralized and electricity-driven everything, including cars, technologies, home heat and appliances, means the electricity can be turned off centrally if we don't comply.[205] New York State has quarantine camps, where it can hold you or your child there

---

[202] Eugenics information and historical figures who have supported it. https://allthatsinteresting.com/eugenics-movement#22

[203] Plandemic 3 Documentary, see the chilling quote from an official on page 82.

[204] The Trojan Horse of The digital Panopticon, Interview of Aman Jabbi, on Disobedient, with Peter Arena, https://www.youtube.com/watch?v=p1i3k-zrYWE

[205] Two of the big pushes for global warming remediation are the electrification of all cars and all home heating systems, as well as cook stoves, and lights.

as long as they wish.[206] This entire plan could enslave the entire world population via digital ID's, computer chips under the skin, cell phones and computers, digital bank accounts, censorship, robotic police and aerial drones, that may recharge themselves on the bright new LED lights being installed on telephone poles everywhere. We might be forced to live in "SMART" cities, where we can only use our digital money in a 20 minute radius from where we live, cut off from Nature, from each other and from the rest of the world population. The 5G network's fantastic speed, which includes ground antennas, cell towers and tens of thousands of satellites in the lower atmosphere, makes all this possible, and covers the entire Earth. Food, housing, cars, household goods might be owned by the authorities. "You will own nothing and you will be happy," came straight from the World Economic Forum's Website, (recently removed from the internet). Instead of you being considered innocent and worthy from the start, you will be considered guilty and suspect from the start. You will constantly need to "be verified," meaning to prove your identity and your worthiness to enter buildings, your car, public buildings, libraries, town halls, etc., which encourages the under the skin chip implant for so-called convenience sake (but actually for control's sake). Freedoms of speech, movement, gatherings and other freedoms could be removed and eliminated. Xi Jinping, the Premier of China, is the golden boy of the WEF, he gave the keynote speech in Davos, Switzerland at the gathering of 2023[207] with all the globalist leaders. What is happening in China is scheduled to happen in the US. Klaus Schwab, former Chairman of the World Economic Forum said "China is a role model for the rest of the world."

We are being manipulated, coerced and poisoned. The proliferation of nanoparticles in our environment is through their being added to packaging, food, vaccines, medications, and inhalation via geoengineering, (jet fuel and chem trails) introducing materials into

---

[206] Follow Attorney Bobbie Ann Cox, for more information: https://www.unitingnys.com/
and the https://attorneycox.substack.com/p/got-questions-ive-got-answers?r=2c9g6j&utm_campaign=post&utm_medium=web
[207] Plandemic 3: link:https://plandemicseries.com/

our bodies without our consent. Graphene Oxide[208] a substance that creates the symptoms of Covid-19, has been discovered in masks, testing swabs and vaccine injections. Humans may be remotely influenced to do things they wouldn't ordinarily do via these mechanisms when the nano particles self form into wire-like segments under the influence of wifi and 5G. Artificial Intelligence[209] is being developed rapidly and there are no controls on its use and or its programming. Technology also creates artificial "thought fields" to influence us, and subliminal messaging to influence our thoughts. **It sounds far fetched, until you find out that it isn't.** This frame work for our lives is being normalized and defended as necessary, using the guise of global warming, equality, racial justice, and other key words that effectively silence any discussion or further investigation. The people in charge of these changes wish to be 'Masters of the world.' (See footnote 115 on pg. 83.)

Link to information on the testing being done to satellites beaming microwave energy on to Earth: https://www.rfsafe.com/cell-towers-in-space-what-cities-will-starlink-irradiate-with-potentially-dangerous-microwaves-from-space/

* * * * * * * * * * * * * *

THE HIPPOCRATIC OATH taken by Medical Doctors (from Wikipedia). ***Amended in 2017***

I swear to fulfill, to the best of my ability and judgment, this covenant:

I will respect the hard-won scientific gains of those physicians in whose steps I walk, and gladly share such knowledge as is mine with those who are to follow.

---

[208] Graphene Oxide poisoning provides the Covid-19 symptoms. It has been found in masks, swabs for Covid-tests, and in vaccines: .*Pfzer, Astrazeneca, Moderna and Janssen.* https://www.orwell.city/2021/07/COMUSAV-CONUVIVE.html this English speaking source reported on the findings from "La Quinta Columna" in Argentina.

[209] See a proposed Code of Ethics for Artificial Intelligence in the appendix.

I will apply, for the benefit of the sick, all measures [that] are required, avoiding those twin traps of over-treatment and therapeutic nihilism.

I will remember that there is art to medicine as well as science, and that warmth, sympathy, and understanding may outweigh the surgeon's knife or the chemist's drug.

I will not be ashamed to say "I know not", nor will I fail to call in my colleagues when the skills of another are needed for a patient's recovery.

I will respect the privacy of my patients, for their problems are not disclosed to me that the world may know. Most especially must I tread with care in matters of life and death. If it is given me to save a life, all thanks. But it may also be within my power to take a life; this awesome responsibility must be faced with great humbleness and awareness of my own frailty. Above all, I must not play at God.

I will remember that I do not treat a fever chart, a cancerous growth, but a sick human being, whose illness may affect the person's family and economic stability. My responsibility includes these related problems, if I am to care adequately for the sick.

I will prevent disease whenever I can, for prevention is preferable to cure.

I will remember that I remain a member of society, with special obligations to all my fellow human beings, those sound of mind and body as well as the infirm.

If I do not violate this oath, may I enjoy life and art, respected while I live and remembered with affection thereafter. May I always act so as to preserve the finest traditions of my calling and may I long experience the joy of healing those who seek my help.

* * * * * * * * * * * * * *

THE HOPI PROPHECY

We are the Ones We've Been Waiting For (By Hopi Elder)

You have been telling people that this is the Eleventh Hour, now you must go back and tell the people that this is the Hour. And there are things to be considered…

Where are you living? What are you doing? What are your relationships? Are you in right relation? Where is your water? Know your garden. It is time to speak your truth. Create your community. Be good to each other. And do not look outside yourself for your leader.

Then he clasped his hands together, smiled, and said, "This could be a good time! There is a river flowing now very fast. It is so great and swift that there are those who will be afraid. They will try to hold on to the shore. They will feel they are being torn apart and will suffer greatly. Know the river has its destination. The elders say we must let go of the shore, push off into the middle of the river, keep our eyes open, and our heads above the water. And I say, see who is in there with you and celebrate. At this time in history, we are to take nothing personally, least of all ourselves. For the moment that we do, our spiritual growth and journey come to a halt. The time of the lone wolf is over. Gather yourselves! Banish the word 'struggle' from your attitude and your vocabulary. All that we do now must be done in a sacred manner and in celebration. We are the ones we've been waiting for.

* * * * * * * * * * * * * *

THE TEN POINTS OF THE NUREMBERG CODE (From Wikipedia)

The ten points of the code were given in the section of the judge's verdict entitled "Permissible Medical Experiments": In response to the trials of Nazi German Medical Doctors that had experimented on human subjects. (I lived across the street from a man who, as a child, had his voice box removed by the Nazis.)

- The voluntary consent of the human subject is absolutely essential. This means that the person involved should have legal capacity to give consent; should be so situated as to be able to exercise free power of choice, without the intervention of any element of force, fraud, deceit, duress, overreaching, or other ulterior form of constraint or coercion; and should have sufficient knowledge and comprehension of the elements of the subject matter involved as to enable him to make an understanding and enlightened decision. This latter element requires that before the acceptance of an affirmative decision by the experimental subject there should be made known to him the nature, duration, and purpose of the experiment; the method and means by which it is to be conducted; all inconveniences and hazards reasonably to be expected; and the effects upon his health or person which may possibly come from his participation in the experiment. The duty and responsibility for ascertaining the quality of the consent rests upon each individual who initiates, directs, or engages in the experiment. It is a personal duty and responsibility which may not be delegated to another with impunity.
- The experiment should be such as to yield fruitful results for the good of society, unprocurable by other methods or means of study, and not random and unnecessary in nature.
- The experiment should be so designed and based on the results of animal experimentation and a knowledge of the natural history of the disease or other problem under study that the anticipated results will justify the performance of the experiment.
- The experiment should be so conducted as to avoid all unnecessary physical and mental suffering and injury.
- No experiment should be conducted where there is an *a priori* reason to believe that death or disabling injury will occur; except, perhaps, in those experiments where the experimental physicians also serve as subjects.

- The degree of risk to be taken should never exceed that determined by the humanitarian importance of the problem to be solved by the experiment.
- Proper preparations should be made and adequate facilities provided to protect the experimental subject against even remote possibilities of injury, disability, or death.
- The experiment should be conducted only by scientifically qualified persons. The highest degree of skill and care should be required through all stages of the experiment of those who conduct or engage in the experiment.
- During the course of the experiment the human subject should be at liberty to bring the experiment to an end if he has reached the physical or mental state where continuation of the experiment seems to him to be impossible.
- During the course of the experiment the scientist in charge must be prepared to terminate the experiment at any stage, if he has probable cause to believe, in the exercise of the good faith, superior skill and careful judgment required of him that a continuation of the experiment is likely to result in injury, disability, or death to the experimental subject.

* * * * * * * * * * * * * *

DOCUMENTARIES AND OTHER REFERENCE MATERIALS

5G From Space, The Role of 5G Satellites, https://www.nokia.com/thought-leadership/articles/5g-space-satellites/ Info on 5G satellites. Pg 28

A Call To Humanity, the interview with Oracle Girl mentioned in Ch. IV, https://www.oraclegirl.org/library/a-call-to-humanity

Emotional Transformation, Learn to Speak the Language of Creation, Hope Mauran, 2005, audio and CD, free to download from https://www.freedomsart.com/emotional-transformation

Del Bigtree, and Coin Bureau, with Guy https://www.youtube.com/watch?v=0wxY1sojA6A,

Died Suddenly https://rumble.com/v1wac7i-world-premier-died-suddenly.html Directed by Matthew Skow and Nicholas Stumphauzer.

Dr Bret Weinstein and Tucker Carlson agree with RFK Jr. on this, https://www.youtube.com/watch?v=mtiUm3fFcs4 (short 2 minute version) https://tuckercarlson.com/the-tucker-carlson-encounter-bret-weinstein/ (60 min. version)

Everyone has been Graphenated, The Vaccine is a directed Bio Weapon, with Dr Robert Young.I nterview on BeforeItsNews.com, April 18, 2023.

Future Dreaming a beautiful, up lifting and insightful interview of Dr. David Martin, filmed in Antarctica https://www.davidmartin.world/future-dreaming/

"Never Again Is Now Global," a documentary by Vera Sharav, on the parallels of the Holocaust and the Pandemic by a Jewish survivor. https://live.childrenshealthdefense.org/chd-tv/events/never-again-is-**now-global/**

Notice that the Davos Conference and WEF employees, are to be flown only by Unvaccinated pilots, because the "safety of our members is no 1 priority." https://www.australiannationalreview.com/health/wef-hires-unvaccinated-pilots-to-fly-them-into-davos-safety-of-our-members-is-no-1-priority/

PEACE PILGRIM: An American Sage Who Walked Her Talk, (1Hour) https://www.youtube.com/watch?v=6ySs2rLcPhU

Plandemic1 https://plandemicseries.com/plandemic-1/

Plandemic2 InDOCTORnation, https://plandemicseries.com/watch-the-great-awakening-movie/

Plandemic 3: The Great Awakening free on https://plandemicseries.com/

Rosa Koire's Talk about Agenda 21, https://m.youtube.com/watch?v=H-qLUQlmBk4

Scientific Evidence of Metaphysical Truths, the series of four talks by Marc Newkirk are available for free on his son Ross's website, ***www.ConsciousTechnologiesllc.com.***

The Science of Natural Law. Mark Passio's Documentary, Does our knowledge or ignorance of these laws impact our collective freedom as a species? In this one-of-a-kind feature documentary film, Mark Passio will explore these questions, and our current understanding of Universal forces that affect the daily lives of each and every one of us. https://onegreatworknetwork.com/mark-passio/mark-passio-the-science-of-natural-law

The Trojan Horse of the Digital Panopticon, Amman Jabbi, https://www.youtube.com/watch?v=pli3k-zrYWE the interview that inspired the surveillance camera brochure mentioned in Chapter V, Freedom from Fear.

The Astounding Convergence of Physics and Metaphysics (2015), Marc Newkirk, a series of 4 talks offered on conscious technologies website, https://www.conscioustechnologiesllc.com/

The Disclosure Project, https://disclosureprojects.com/ and **The Lost Century**, https://www.thelostcenturyfilm.com/ by Dr Stephen Greer.

The Vaccine Death Report, Evidence of millions of deaths and serious adverse events resulting from the experimental COVID-19 injections BY DAVID JOHN SORENSEN & DR. VLADIMIR ZELENKO MD VERSION **1.0** SEPT. 2021

Thrive, and **Thrive II,** This Is What It Takes by Kimberly Carter Gamble and Foster Gamble. wwwThriveOn.com

Totality of Evidence on Covid-19, Ed Dowd's website https://totalityofevidence.com/

Weaponization of Coronavirus: When Nature is Conscripted to Harm, David Martin's speech at the Weston A Price Foundation https://www.bitchute.com/video/fHhniBm4cyiM/

What are all those Surveillance Cameras *really for? This flyer outlines what is currently being implemented by the United Nations, World Economic Forum, World Health Organization and Global Corporations, their comprehensive plan for 2030 is called: THE GREAT RESET... Are you aware of it?* A brochure available to read and download at https://www.freedomsart.com/offerings

Why Co_2 is not the Enemy they Want you to Believe. Patrick Moore, Greenpeace Co-Founder's talk. https://www.youtube.com/watch?v=TclmRoTGsO4

BIBLIOGRAPHY

Author not named, 2012, Handbook for the New Paradigm, Idaho, Bridger house Publishers, Inc.

Author not named, 2012, Embracing The Rainbow, Idaho, Bridger house Publishers, Inc.

Author not named, 2012, Becoming, Idaho, Bridger house Publishers, Inc.

Bartholomew, Alick, 2003, **Hidden Nature, The Startling Insights of Viktor Schauberger,** Kempton Illinois, Adventures Unlimited Press.

Benz, Inelia, 2022, **Earth Files**, published by Inelia Benz.

Dhanesvara Das**,** 2009- 2010, **Lessons in Spiritual Economics**, from the Bhagavad-Gita, Part one, available from www.spiritual-econ.com.

Freeland, Elana, 2021, **Geoengineered Transhumanism, How the Environment Has Been Weaponized By Chemicals, Electromagnetism and Nanotechnology For Synthetic Biology**, Elana Freeland.

Hall, Manly, 2015, **The Pineal Gland: The eye of God**, Comprising Ch XVI of *Man: The Grand Symbol of the Mysteries,* Mansfield Centre, CT., Martino Publishing.

Holliwell, Raymond, 2004, **Working With the Law, 11 Truth Principles for Successful Living**, Camarillo, CA, DeVorss Publications.

Icke, David, 2023, **The Dream, The extraordinary revelation of who we are and where we are,** Derby U.K., Ickonic Publishing.

Jenny, Hans, 1974, revised 2001, **Cymatics,** Newmarket NH, MACROmedia publishing.

Karim, Dr. Ibrahim, PhD-Tech.Sc., ETH-ZH, 2022, **Hidden Reality, The BioGeometry Physics of Quality, The Science of Subtle Energy and Life Force**, Dr. Ibrahim F. Karim Biogeometry Energy Systems Ltd Publisher.

Kelly, Penny, 2022, **The Revival, Path to a New Earth/New Human**, Lawton Michigan, Lily Hill Publishing.

Kennedy, Robert F. Jr., and Hooker, Brian, 2023, **Vax-Unvax, Let the Science Speak,** Simon and Schuster.

Mander, Jerry, 1992, **In the Absence Of The Sacred, The Failure of Technology & the Survival of the Indian Nations**, San Francisco, Sierra Club Books.

Matoushek, MPH, PT, Nicole, 2009, **What I Forgot The Day I Was Born,** USA, Xlibris Corporation.

Mauran, Hope Ives, 2011, **Be The Second Coming, Guidebook to the Embodiment of the Christ Within: a personal journey our collective destiny**, Bloomington, IN, Balboa Press.

Mauran, Hope Ives, 2016, **The Key To Love, A Teaching From The Beings Of Light,** NY**,** Legwork Team Publishing.

McTaggart, Lynne, 2017, **The Power of Eight**, NY, NY, Astria Paperback.

Megre, Vladimir, 2005, **The New Civilization,** book 8 part 1, of The Ringing Cedars of Russia series, Hawaii, Ringing Cedars Press.

Megre, Vladimir, 2006, **Co-creation**, The Ringing Cedars of Russia series book 4, Hawaii, Ringing Cedars Press..

Mercola, Dr. Joseph, and Cummins, Ronnie, 2021, **The Truth About COVID-19, exposing The Great Reset, Lockdowns, Vaccine passports, and the New Normal, Why we Must Unite in a Global Movement for Health and Freedom**, White River Jct. Vt, Chelsea Green Publishing.

Northrup, Christiane, M.D., 2021, **A mom's guide to the COVID shot,** Oklahoma, Thrive Publishing.

Parry, Glen Aparicio, 2020, **Original Politics, Making America Sacred Again**, New York, Select Books.

Peace Pilgrim, **Peace Pilgrim, Her life and Work in Her Own Words,** 1982, Santa Fe, NM, Ocean Tree Books.

Schermerhorn, Lisa B., 2022, **In Every Belief is a Lie,** Lisa B. Shermerhorn.

Schucman, Helen, 2017, **A Course In Miracles, Circle of Atonement**, Circle of Atonement, Inc..

Steiner, Rudolph, 2003, **The Reappearance of Christ in the Etheric, a Collection of Lectures on The Second Coming of Christ**, Massachusetts. USA, Steiner Books.

Swartz, James, 2014, **The Essence of Enlightenment**, Boulder Colorado, Sentient Publications.

Tellinger, Michael, 2013, **Ubuntu Contributionism, A Blueprint For Human Prosperity**, South Africa, Zulu Planet Publishers.

The Findhorn Community, 1975, **The Findhorn Garden, Pioneering a new Vision of man and Nature in Cooperation**, USA, Harper & Row Publishers.

Tompkins, Peter, 2009, **The Secret Life of Nature, Living in Harmony with the Hidden world of Nature Spirits, from Fairies to Quarks**, New Dlehi, Rup Publications, India Pvt. Ltd..

Wappnick, PhD., Kenneth, 2021, **Absence From Felicity, The Story of Helen Schucman and Her Scribing of A COURSE IN MIRACLES**, Nevada, Foundation for A Course in Miracles.

Webb, David Rodgers, 2023, **The Great Taking**, David Rogers Webb, printed through Lulu; free e-book download: https://thegreattaking.com/read-online-or-download

Yogananda, Paramahansa, 2005, **Harmonizing Physical, Mental & Spiritual Methods of Healing**, Paramahansa Yogananda, How to Live Series No 1707, Self Realization Fellowship.

Young, Dr. Robert. O, PhD. And T.M. Ballantyne, 2023, **TRUTH vs. Deception, Liberty vs. Tyranny, Covid 19 – Fact vs. Fiction**, USA, Ballantyne Books.

Additional Sources:

Hoffman, Hallock**, 1967, The Quaker Dialogue**, a chapter from a book entitled *"The Civilization of the Dialogue"* a publication of the Center for the Study of Democratic Institutions.

Kimmerer, Robin Wall, April 2016, interview in The Sun magazine, called **Two Ways of Knowing, Robin "Wall Kimmerer On Scientific And Native American Views Of The Natural World**, by Leath Tonino.

Mauran, Hope, 2005, **Emotional Transformation,** *Learn To Speak The Language of Creation,* a CD, and it is available to download for free online at *www.FreedomsArt.com.*

Mauran, Hope, 2023, **It was a Dark and Stormy Night on Planet Earth, and the People Said "No More!"** Inspirational Booklet that inspired this book to be written. https://uploads.striklinglycdn.com/files/3833ea8d-7e62-44e6-ae0b-219e8630371a/DarkAndStormyNight.pdf?t=1706107932&id=4099990

Newkirk, Marc, **Scientific Evidence of Metaphysical Truths,** the series of four talks is available for free on his son Ross's website www.ConsciousTechnologiesllc.com

* * * * * * * * * * * *

ABOUT THE AUTHOR

Photo by BARRIE FISHER PHOTO

After a channeled reading in 1998 said that I was a psychic and an artist, I began communicating with my spirit guides and painting. I call myself a translator of wisdom from other dimensions, and have written four books as a result: The Key To Love, A Teaching from The Beings of Light for an Enlightened Reality of Earth (2016); Being The Miracle Of Love, Conversations With Jesus (2013); Be the Second Coming, Guidebook to the Embodiment of the Christ Within: a Personal Journey, Our Collective Destiny (2012), and Where the Wisdom Lies: A Message from Nature's Small Creatures (2006). I have also recorded an audio CD, entitled Emotional Transformation: Learn to Speak the Language of Creation (2005). I am grateful to share these inspiring messages of non-duality and unconditional love.

My birth name is Hope, my given name is Freedom. Given by my higher self, a reminder to me and to all of us, that we are free and powerful beings already and always.

Some of my artwork, which I describe as "eco-spiritual modified landscapes", guided drawings and an illustration of the spiritual journey may be seen on the website. Www.FreedomsArt.com